The Hijacking
of Christianity in the
Age of Trump

D1739262

Dean Krippaehne

Published by RMC Publishing
21040 Fifth Avenue South
Seattle, Washington 98198 USA
www.deankrippaehne.net

Edited by Kelsey Krippaehne

Library of Congress cataloging data available upon
request.

ISBN: 9798634646770

CONTENTS

Preface

The Hijacking of Christianity is nothing new. Even before the Bible was fully assembled there were forces attempting to usurp the emerging Christian religion in order to obtain political power, secure personal gain, or to profit from other self-serving agendas. The Crusades, the selling of indulgences, the justification of slavery, the support of the Nazi party leading into the Holocaust, and denying women voting rights are all well-documented historical examples of certain persons or entities within Christian power circles spinning, twisting, propagating falsehoods, and outright lying about the meaning and intent of Biblical scripture to accomplish their goals.

In other words, the hijacking of Christianity is as old as Christianity itself.

This book does not attempt to re-litigate the past but rather focuses solely on the hijacking of Christianity in the modern age, specifically during the campaign and presidency of Donald Trump. These pages will spotlight statements, assertions and actions made by individuals in Evangelical Church leadership who have abused their power positions by misusing scripture. While pinpointing personal motive is always difficult, it is reasonable to assume that much of their conduct has been driven by one or more of the following: gaining political influence, self-aggrandizement, control of narrative, dissemination of falsehoods, or actual belief in misguided Biblical interpretations. Whatever their motives, the unfortunate consequence has been the sowing of seeds for dangerous group-think patterns to emerge, grow and flourish.

Throughout these pages I will seek to call out various hijackings and point the way toward Biblical interpretations much more in keeping with the teachings of Jesus, His infinite wisdom and Grace, and His welcoming invitation to all humankind. Let me assure you the overwhelming motive in this narrative is love. God's love. Love for the Almighty and Love for the neighbor - you. It is in this Spirit of Love that I will endeavor to intercede on behalf of the voiceless many, by challenging the megaphoned few.

My great hope is that through these writings some who have been led astray may find their way back to the heart of Jesus. And that others may gather strength in the knowledge that God is, indeed, the God of mercy and Grace who loves and welcomes all people to His table. I pray, too, that those Christian leaders who may have lost their way will somehow, some way and someday have an authentic "come back to Jesus" moment.

I hope that day is today.

Introduction

Almost every day I wrestle with whether or not to speak out about those who misrepresent Jesus in the age of Trump. I wrestle in part because I don't need or want the blowback that can happen when one speaks out in this way. I also wrestle because I am caught between the voice of Jesus Christ saying things like, *"Turn the other cheek, love one another, be patient, kind, etc..."* and a couple of other voices I respect who offer conflicting axioms. Dietrich Bonhoeffer, for one, who lived in the dark and troubled times of the Third Reich, offered this warning as he witnessed the nazification of Germany: *"Silence in the face of evil is itself evil: God will not hold us guiltless. Not to speak is to speak. Not to act is to act."* And, of course, the voice of Martin Luther and his "95 Theses" which called out certain corrupt practices and theology of the Catholic Church in the early 1500s. Voicing those criticisms made him a seminal figure in the Protestant Reformation. It also got him excommunicated from the church.

And so I wrestle. Much of the time I do not speak. Sometimes I do. Now is one of those times when I am speaking up and speaking out. To be quiet in the face of what I have heard and witnessed from more than a few powerful Evangelical Christian leaders these last years is unacceptable. To remain quiet, I have concluded, would be tantamount to condoning or agreeing with their twisted version of Jesus's words. Hence, I lift my voice.

But I do so with hope. The hope of enlightenment. The hope that my Evangelical friends will push politics aside and hear the voice of Jesus in my words. The hope that wisdom and civility will prevail. The hope that although some Christians and I have dramatically differing views on Biblical interpretations, we can come to some consensus on a few core values of Jesus and take a cue from former Supreme Court Justice Scalia and Supreme Court Justice Ginsburg who were diametrically opposed on many issues, yet remained great friends. I hope for unity. Unity in disagreement. Unity in Christ. I hope.

Author's Note

I should start out by saying that I'm a church guy. A follower of Jesus. Technically speaking, I am a Christian, but I usually refer to myself simply as "a follower of and believer in Jesus." More on that later. I have been a worship leader and worship pastor at an ELCA Christian church for over 25 years. I love the church community and have been lucky enough to have served in one that is filled with God's Grace and seeks to welcome and be inclusive of all people.

Let me be clear that although my tone may *seem* at times in this book to be condemning the Christian Church and Evangelical Christianity, I am not. Both, at their best, are wonderful tools people can use to help them walk in a full, meaningful and complete relationship with Jesus. However, both, at their worst, can be a hammer, not only damaging people and leading them down a dangerous and destructive path but, indeed, nailing the Spirit of God to a cross of crucifixion.

I trust that these pages will help those reading to better identify Churches and Christian institutions when and where they have gone wrong. And that if you should ever find yourself in the midst of a harmful, abusive community, I pray that you will either strive to change it or flee to the safety of a Grace-filled house of worship.

In the Beginning...

"These aren't people. These are animals." - Donald J. Trump

"Love your neighbor as yourself." - Jesus

Hijacking Christianity

God's will through Jesus Christ is pretty clear.

Love everybody.

What God *doesn't* say is, *"Love the ones you choose,"* or *"only love the ones who agree with you,"* or *"only love the ones who have a particular religious point of view, or come from a particular country."* Nope. God's will is that you and I love *everybody.* Our neighbors. And every human in the entire *world* is our neighbor.

Got it?

But what about the people we don't like very much?

God often allows difficult people to enter into our lives for the purpose of showing us how *we* sometimes behave towards God. We may be loving, caring, giving and delightful to everyone around us but still sometimes act or think in ways that can be frustrating, difficult or irritating to God. Thank God (literally) for forgiving us for this inner and sometimes outer misbehavior.

But let there be no mistake: God's will is that we love one another. Even when it is difficult. Any doctrine that is in opposition to this all-encompassing *love for neighbor* is in opposition to God. This is the God of Christianity. This is the God we know through Jesus Christ. This *is* the Word and will of Jesus Christ.

Many Christians are turning a blind eye to this fundamental reality of Jesus. They are opting not to act in loving ways towards everyone. They are also openly supporting politicians who continually engage in non-loving words and actions *without calling those politicians out.* Instead of holding them accountable, they have been justifying these politician's heedless behaviors by misusing Bible passages. I can only guess they are doing this because they either believe in a theology of exclusion and belittlement, or because they are serving their own personal or political agenda.

When people twist the meaning of scripture they are acting in accordance with *their own* will - not the will of God through Jesus Christ. When Christian leaders openly conduct themselves in this way I call it "hijacking Christianity." That is to say they are using Christianity in a manner contrary to the teachings of Jesus and projecting a false image of Christ and Christianity to the world.

In the age of Donald Trump this type of exploitation has been magnified tenfold. Politics have become tribal and emotions are running at a fever pitch. (We'll dig into some of the reasons *why* later in this book.) This tribalism is causing politics to bleed into

Evangelical Christianity and vice versa. As Christians we need to always make the *loving of **all** people* our primary message and stop selectively using or contorting scripture to advance our own agenda.

Many are stumbling and falling into this dark and twisted trap. Consequently, a dangerous version of Christianity - and more importantly, a false representation of Jesus - is being projected out unto the world.

Hiking the Treacherous Trail

Today I am hiking up in the mountains. The trail I'm on, if you want to call it that, is basically a haphazard assembly of rocks. There are small rocks, medium size rocks, bigger rocks, and boulders the size of cars. Some of the rocks have sharp, jagged edges. They would be difficult enough to navigate on a normal day, but a light rain fell last night which has made their bare faces wet, slippery and treacherous.

Of course, it doesn't help that as I'm hiking I am speaking these words into my smartphone. Yeah, smart phone, dumb person.

Back to the hike.

The rocks and small boulders are broken up by an occasional tree root. Today they are evil tree roots. As anyone who has hiked before knows, a slippery tree root can lay you out flat in two seconds. You've got to be utterly cautious every step of the way in these conditions lest you fall and injure yourself out in the middle of nowhere.

Trust me, I have broken my leg while out on a hike before. (No, I wasn't talking into my smartphone when I did it.) It wasn't a fun situation to be in. Every year there are people in these mountains who need to be rescued. Occasionally someone will even tragically fall to their death up here. One needs to keep their eyes focused on the trail in order to avoid all the sharp rocks and the occasional deadly tree root.

The religious world is much like this mountain trail.

A vigilant eye is required to avoid potential pitfalls.

Sadly, there are certain conservative Christian leaders and teachers who will say things that can throw us off the path. Things that can trip us up and may make us fall. Many of them will use false and dangerous interpretations of scripture to justify their personal positions and convictions. And just like you and I can become physically damaged from falling on a slippery rock, so too can we become spiritually, emotionally or psychologically damaged by slipping on faulty teaching or preaching.

We need to beware of those who justify statements and actions of their favorite political leaders by twisting the words of Christ. We need to be especially cautious of those who justify statements and actions of political leaders by *cherry-picking* scripture to support their claims and agenda. This practice is what I call religious *fake news*. It is misleading and dangerous.

Often the only way to identify these imposters is to stay close to Christ.

We will examine some of this misuse of scripture in statements made by a few Evangelical Christian leaders later in this book. But first I want to go back to the beginning. I want us to take a brief look at how and where the current hijacking of Christianity may have gotten started.

Let us proceed.

The Moral Majority

For all of the great things that have been born out of Christianity, and there are many, it also has a tremendously appalling side to its history.

From Constantine to the Inquisitions. From the Crusades to the Salem Witch Trials. From the support of slavery to denying women the right to individual liberty. When the Christian church and politics have mixed in a particular way, it has produced some of the most atrocious human behaviors and consequences in all of history.

Many of the Old Testament justifications used throughout Christianity's violent past completely disregarded the primary call from Jesus in the New Testament - *to love one another*. In much the same way, many of those same justifications are being used today to distort and twist God's Word, sometimes entirely ignoring the New Testament's message of peace, unity and love.

One can easily trace the roots of modern day anti-Jesus behaviors by some wearing the Christian name all the way back to Constantine, but for the purposes of this book we need only go back as far as the now defunct Moral Majority.

The Moral Majority was founded by Baptist minister Jerry Falwell in the late 1970's. Its primary objective was to organize and mobilize conservative Christians as a powerful political force with the goal of bringing those supporting the Moral Majority's version of morality into political power.

Indeed, they succeeded in their goals. Throughout its active years the Moral Majority enjoyed numerous political successes with local and state level candidates as well as being a prime voting bloc in the landslide victory of Ronald Regan over Jimmy Carter in the 1980 Presidential elections.

One of the problems with the Moral Majority's church and politics marriage was their tap-dancing around and playing games with the First Amendment's concept regarding *the separation of church and state.*

To refresh our high-school civics memory, let's take a quick look back at Thomas Jefferson's understanding of The First Amendment of the United States Constitution.

> *"Congress shall make no law respecting an establishment of religion, or prohibiting the free exercise thereof..."* This, he said, built a *"wall of separation of church and state"* along with Article Six which specifies that, *"no religious Test shall ever be required as a Qualification to any Office or public Trust under the United States."*

In a nutshell, Jefferson's understanding of the First Amendment was that it guarantees that the government does not show preference to any particular religion and that the government does not expropriate any individual's ability to exercise religion. In other words, *the church will not rule over the state, and the state cannot rule over the church.*

It needs to be said that many on the religious-right dispute this intent.

Not me.

I respectfully disagree with the religious-right on this matter.

I think the founders of the United States knew *exactly* what they were doing by keeping separate church and state.

In addition to Jefferson's understanding, John Dickinson, one of the Founding Fathers, wrote in 1768:

"Religion and Government are certainly very different Things, instituted for different Ends; the design of one being to promote our temporal Happiness; the design of the other to procure the Favour of God, and thereby the Salvation of our Souls. While these are kept distinct and apart, the Peace and welfare of Society is preserved, and the Ends of both are answered. By mixing them together, feuds, animosities and persecutions have been raised, which have deluged the World in Blood, and disgraced human Nature."

Most certainly Mr. Dickinson was of the opinion that in order to have a respectable, ethical and effective government it was essential that religion and politics be divided.

Add to all this the fact that Jesus Christ was not concerned with aligning Himself to any particular government. As Jesus said, *"My Kingdom is not of this world" (John 18:36), "For indeed, the kingdom of God is within you." (Luke 17:21 NKJV)*

All of the relational teachings of Jesus Christ focus on the heart, mind, soul and actions of the *individual.* And on one's relationship with others. Not on any particular government or country.

Some say that when Jesus spoke the words, *"seek first the Kingdom" (Matthew 6:33),* He was talking about establishing a government here on earth. Nothing could be further from the truth. The Kingdom which Jesus was referring to, the one He longs for us to enter into, is the Spiritual Kingdom of God that He will build in our hearts and minds. Again, as Jesus said, *"the kingdom of God is within you."*

Please note that I am not being naive in thinking that Christians don't at times seek to sway governmental policy when they feel an injustice has occurred. Christian *values* of social justice and integrity often influence government policy as was the case when Dr. Martin Luther King Jr. fought for Civil Rights. But Dr. King was not advocating for a Christian government. Indeed, *Morality,* which has its roots in religion, influences both our lives and the political spectrum. However, this particular kind of influence is not what I intend to illuminate in this book. Jesus had no intention of being a government. *"Give to Caesar what is Caesar's, and to God what is God's." - Jesus (Matthew 22:21 BSB)*

The only government Jesus hopes for is His Spirit governing our hearts. The heart of the individual. And a collective of individuals are to be His church. A church with no borders, no boundaries and no walls that exclude or divide.

Although The Moral Majority has long been defunct, its roots, influence and power have not only survived but thrived and metastasized within the minds and teachings of many conservative Evangelical Christians and political leaders, as well as their congregations and constituents.

I believe the permeation of the Moral Majority's influence (and their push to make the United States a Christian nation) has shown itself to have materialized and mutated in a powerful and disturbing way in the Age of Trump. With the overwhelming and ever-increasing number of falsehoods* stated and tweeted by Donald Trump we are, indeed, living in an Orwellian era of *"don't believe your eyes and ears"* fully supported and enabled by some in the conservative Christian Church. Consequently, I would assert that in the public eye Christianity has been and continues to be *hijacked* away from Jesus Christ by those with personal and political agendas.

Let the following pages speak credence to my contention.

Building Walls

"Whatever you do to the least of these you do to me." - Jesus

I have a few questions and maybe some answers.

Is there an immigration challenge at the southern border of the United States?

Yes.

In the last four decades has the United States figured out how to meet this challenge?

No.

What does Jesus think about building walls that keep the needy from getting help?

I'm pretty sure He doesn't like it.

Here's a Biblical quiz question: Did Jesus ever instruct His followers to build a wall for the purpose of keeping people away from Him, His love and His Kingdom? No. Jesus never says anything remotely like that in the Bible. The idea that Jesus would build a wall to keep people from Him and His love is a ludicrous idea. Jesus *always* welcomed *all* people.

How about those who are desperate and hungry, sick and poor, those who are fleeing violence and or corrupt governments - what does Jesus say about them? Did Jesus say, "Don't take care of the sick and most certainly don't take care of the poor?" Nope. And to the ones fleeing violence, did Jesus say, "Ah, what the heck, let them get killed?" That's a double-down nope. This is not the way Jesus responds to those in need. In fact, it is completely contrary to the Word of God and contrary to the heart of Jesus.

Let the following story bring to light this great Truth.

Rich Man

There's a story in The Bible about two neighbors. One is a very, very rich man. He has everything he needs in abundance and then some. The other man is a very poor, sick, hungry and desperate man named Lazarus.

In this Bible story, the poor, hungry and sick Lazarus comes to the door of his rich neighbor. He needs a little help. He is not asking for much, just a few food scraps from the rich man's table. Something the rich man would probably give to his dog or maybe even throw away. But instead of welcoming his neighbor in need, the rich man gives Lazarus nothing.

Well, as fate would have it, the poor, hungry Lazarus dies and goes up to heaven where he is finally comforted, fed, healed and taken care of. The rich man also dies, but he goes to a place where he is suffering. Every single minute of every hour of every day, the rich man is now in misery. Total agony. And although the rich man wants to get across the wide chasm that now separates him from a peaceful, comforted Lazarus, there is no possible way for him to get there.

The rich man begs Abraham (A Hebrew patriarch revered in Christianity, Judaism and Islam) to send a sign or a signal to alert his family to the eternal suffering that awaits them if they don't become more generous in opening their doors to their neighbors in need. Abraham tells the rich man that God has already given his family members plenty of signs and shown them great miracles. And that sending any more would not soften their hardened hearts.

Yikes.

This story is a warning to us all.

Especially to all of us who live in the United States, a country of great abundance. The United States is the rich man while much of the rest of the world is Lazarus. Right now poor, hungry immigrants are knocking at the door of our Southern border. The only question is this: will we open our door and give them some scraps from our table of abundance - or not?

And God is waiting to see what our answer will be.

Wow!

Do you get it?

Can you see the way in which God wants us to care for those in need?

Now let me be clear. I'm not advocating that we impose the will of Jesus upon our government like the Moral Majority did. That would violate the "separation of church and state" intent of our nation's founders. Instead, I'm using this story to point out the compassion that Jesus wants to put in each of our hearts and the loving action He would have each of His followers take. Do you see the difference?

Jesus doesn't build walls that keep people out. He builds bridges. Bridges that welcome people. Bridges of hope. Bridges of love. Bridges of caring and bridges of kindness.

And the bridges Jesus builds are relationships. Loving and caring relationships with *all* people.

I can fully understand why a government needs to monitor and judiciously screen refugees who enter into its country. Yes, you need to identify anyone who may have dangerous or criminal intentions. You need to find ways to pay for the care that you freely give away. And, of course, a country needs to document people for the sake of running a functional government. But that is not what I'm talking about here.

What I want to shine a light on is how a few Christian leaders and Christians in general react to some of the policies their government in the Age of Trump is promoting. Don't get me wrong - *you can support either major political party in the United States and still be a Christian.* You can support them because you agree with their overall domestic and foreign policies. You can support them for any reason you like.

But when a Christian leader - *one who has brought politics to the pulpit* - witnesses his or her political party carry out certain actions contrary to the heart of Jesus, it is incumbent upon them not to lie about it. If you are walking with Jesus you cannot simply sweep something contrary to His nature under the rug. You must speak the Truth and speak up for Jesus.

As I've stated, a follower of Jesus may support *any* political party they wish because they believe in that party's overall platform and philosophy. But if the political party they support advocates building walls to keep people in need from safety and shelter, then they must make it known that denying men, women and children who are sick, hungry, poor and fleeing persecution is contrary to the teachings of the One they call Lord. This is something all who have the Holy Spirit dwelling within their heart should have no question about. Even setting aside Christianity, people of all religions throughout the world would agree that withholding help from those in desperate need is an inhumane thing to do.

And yet we have religious leaders who, along with many of their congregational members, talk as if keeping out the needy by building a great wall along the southern border of the United States is perfectly acceptable to Jesus. It is not.

I'll say it again: ignoring or banning people from the help and care they need is *not* OK with Jesus. This goes to the core of who Jesus is and what He is about. Those who support the building of a wall along the southern border of the United States in order to keep out refugees and immigrants and say they are doing so in the name of Christianity, are indeed *hijacking Christianity* because this is absolutely *not* of Christ. Sadly, thanks to the hijacking of Christianity, this "wall builder Jesus" is the only Jesus some non-Christians will ever see. They see a Jesus who excludes and doesn't care about those in desperate need.

Support the building of a wall to keep out the needy if you must - but doing so in the name of Jesus is akin to hammering another nail through His hand or wrist on the cross.

Why is walling out the needy so anti-Jesus?

First of all, Jesus's great commandment tells us to *love our neighbor*. And who is our neighbor? *Everyone*. Everyone on the planet. Building a wall and keeping out those in need is *not* loving our neighbor. Jesus also said in His parable of the Good Samaritan that the Samaritan was the one who got it right. *(Luke 10:25-37)* The Samaritan was the one who actually helped the person in distress along the side of the road. The others along the road, the ones who saw but didn't help, got it wrong. And Jesus says to you and to me, *"Go and do likewise" (Luke 10:37)*. In essence, *be loving, caring and kind like the Good Samaritan.*

This is as plain as day and as clear as the nose on anyone's face. To avoid helping these refugees along the road of our United States Southern border, or any refugees anywhere, is contrary to the will of Jesus Christ. Again, I want to be clear that the government can do what the people elected it to do (separation of church and state has proven itself to be an imperative for the good of all people), but a follower of Jesus, a Christian, if he or she is doing the will of our Lord, will not support an action denying those in need.

Jesus also said, *"feed my sheep" (John 21:17)*, which means take care of the poor and the sick and the homeless. He did not say "deny my sheep food and build a wall to keep out the sick and the poor and the homeless and the widows and the orphans." And yet there are some Christians who are acting as if this is exactly what Jesus said.

Is there a challenge with immigration at the Southern border of the United States? Yes. Have we figured out how to solve this challenge yet? No. Is building a wall the answer? Maybe, maybe not. I won't weigh in on that political issue. But I will weigh in on this: *Building a wall to keep out the poor, the sick, the needy, the hungry, the widows and the orphans is absolutely not what Jesus would do.*

The Muslim Ban

In January of 2017 the now infamous *Muslim Ban* (Executive Order 13769) was signed by President Donald Trump. It had a brief implementation before it was subsequently rejected by the courts in its original form. Although it wasn't a complete and sweeping ban of Muslims entering the United States, it became known as the *Muslim Ban* in large part due to a statement Donald Trump had made and posted on his campaign website in late 2015. After much condemnation and negative rebuke the statement was taken off of his website. Before it was taken down this statement read:

> *"Donald J. Trump is calling for a total and complete shutdown of Muslims entering the United States until our country's representatives can figure out what the hell is going on."* (Dec. 7, 2015)

I think most reasonable people would agree that this is quite a revealing statement of Donald Trump's *intent*. Sadly, many conservative Evangelical leaders and Evangelicals supported him in part *because* of this statement. This statement also gave great credence to the contention that Executive Order 13769 was intended to give the not so subtle message to the Muslim community that, "you are not welcome here."

In much the same way that building a wall along the southern border to keep people out of the United States is not what Jesus would do, banning people of other countries from entering the United States based solely on their religious belief is likewise absolutely not what Jesus would do. Most certainly our government must be discerning, diligent and cautious about *any* people entering our country. There are always a few who may have nefarious intent. But to paint any particular religion with one broad brush stroke is not something Jesus would ever do.

Jesus welcomes all people to his table. All people. A follower of Christ, at their best, welcomes everyone to their table as well. This includes people of different religions, different beliefs, or people with no spiritual beliefs whatsoever. Nowhere does Jesus say that we should exclude people who are not Christians. In fact, those are the ones we should be welcoming first and foremost. After all, that's what Jesus did.

Let's examine for a moment what Jesus had to say about welcoming people into our home.

> *"When you give a luncheon or dinner, do not invite your friends, your brothers or sisters, your relatives, or your rich neighbors; if you do, they may invite you back and so you will be repaid. **But when you give a banquet, invite the poor, the crippled, the lame, the blind,** and you will be blessed. Although they cannot repay you, you will be repaid at the resurrection of the righteous." (Luke 14: 12-14)*

Back when Jesus was walking the face of the Earth, *no one was a Christian*. Some had other religions or belief systems they followed, and some had no religion at all. Yet He welcomed them. He welcomed them all. So too should we welcome all people - just like Jesus did.

It would probably be a good idea for many of the Christians who supported Donald Trump's Muslim Ban to reacquaint themselves with a lesson that the Apostle Paul taught while speaking to the people of Athens. When Paul went to Athens to spread the love and word of Jesus he saw that the people there worshiped other gods and an "unknown god." However, he didn't ban them from his presence because they worshiped differently. Instead, the very first thing he did was compliment them. *He built a bridge.* He opened the door to a relationship.

"People of Athens! I see that in every way you are very religious. For as I walked around and looked carefully at your objects of worship I even found an altar with this inscription: TO AN UNKNOWN GOD." (Acts 17: 22-23)

He accepted them where they were and then invited them to listen to his story.

Just as Paul wasn't building walls to keep out people of different religions, Jesus certainly wasn't banning people from being near Him. He was trying to draw them closer. *"Come and see" (John 1:39),* *"Come to me, all you that are weary and are carrying heavy burdens, and I will give you rest." (Matthew 11:28),* Jesus says.

Shouldn't we do the same? As followers of Jesus, shouldn't we accept all people where they are and strive to build bridges of love and kindness? Then maybe at some point, if they grow to trust us, they might be interested in hearing our story.

There were many people in Jesus' day who were despised or discarded. People who were summarily disliked and distrusted based on some arbitrary aspect of their being. Many others, including the religious elites, wanted to section them off or ban those "undesirables" from the normal day-to-day walk of life. These despised people included Gentiles and Samaritans and lepers. They also included the blind who were left to beg on the streets and women who were generally viewed as a type of property - all banned from most of the privileges of civilization.

Jesus turned this equation upside down. He welcomed the

Samaritans and the Gentiles. He embraced the lepers and the blind, even providing them with health care by healing them. He spoke to women at a time when men were not allowed to greet women in public - and then went a step further by welcoming these women into His world completely.

The valuing of all human life is a quality that Donald Trump seems to lack. You may have forgotten this, but when Donald Trump was asked during the beginning of his presidential campaign back in late 2015 how to fight ISIS, he said, *"you have to take out their families."* Yeah, you read that right. His opinion was that the way to defeat ISIS was to kill their families. Not only is that absolutely immoral, it is also illegal - a criminal action and a war crime. And yet, some conservative Evangelicals simply brushed those comments aside and gave him their full support. To be perfectly clear, Jesus does not support killing families.

Sometimes Christians get it so painfully backwards. They misunderstand the Word of Christ and the heart of Jesus so profoundly that it boggles the mind. Yes, we should be discerning, perform our due diligence, and keep a watchful eye out for those few people both outside and inside our borders who may be motivated to harm others. But as followers of Christ we should never have an all-encompassing negative view of any people. Jesus values people.

Let us as followers of Christ not succumb to painting everyone of a particular religion, or region, or color, or race, or belief with one broad brushstroke. We should not build high walls to keep them out. Nor should we happily agree with the political clarion call for bans or banishment. Instead we should seek to build bridges of kindness, acceptance and understanding. This is what Jesus did. We who bear His name should do the same.

It grieves me greatly when Christian leaders and their followers support the idea of a ban on Muslims or any other group of people. Let me reiterate: this is contrary to the will of Christ and contrary to the will of God. Furthermore, when they do this publicly or from the podiums at their churches, they have hijacked the Word of Jesus and besmirched the Christian religion.

If you are inclined to support the politicians who promote this type of sweeping ban on a particular peoples, that is your prerogative. However, if you are a *Christian* supporting this type of action, you need to be fully aware that what you are supporting is contrary to the nature of Jesus Christ.

From time to time we all turn our figurative backs on Jesus - if only momentarily - to justify our behaviors, words or actions. At our best we realize the error of our ways and repent. Repent, meaning that we turn away from those errors in judgement and turn back towards our Lord. I pray for those bearing His name who have capitulated to these types of anti-Jesus behaviors. I pray that they will repent.

And...

This country was founded upon the idea that everyone and anyone was welcome here, no matter where they were from. Christianity was founded upon the same principle. That all are welcome to "come and see." That all are welcome in God's Kingdom. No matter what you look like, no matter how you pray, no matter where you are from, no matter how rich or poor you are, no matter how sick or healthy, according to Jesus you are welcome to *come and see.*

It seems that some have wandered far from those ideals, both as Americans in the United States and as Christians. This is sad. Shame on us when we walk away from the principle that all men and women are created equal. And shame on us as Christians when instead of building bridges of welcome we support walls of exclusion. We must do better. We must be better.

Our true calling is not unique. It is the same for each and every person on earth. To love one another.

Relationships

It was Thursday morning.

I was visiting my dad. He was staying at my brother's house. He was dying. My brother had a hospice bed set up in his living room (which had now become a makeshift bedroom). After visiting my dad for an hour or so, I had to leave and go to work. I said to him, "You're not going to like this but I'm going to give you a hug and a kiss." My dad wasn't a hugger or a kisser - ever. So I put my arms around him, gave him a kiss on the side of his face and whispered, "I love you." He smiled and laughed a bit. I think the morphine helped him enjoy the gesture. With that I said, "goodbye, I'll see ya later" and then walked out the door. I never did see him later. He died that night. It was such a little thing – the hug and kiss. But it was such a huge thing. I sure am glad I hugged and kissed him and said "I love you" that Thursday morning.

The essence of life is relationships. The essence of Jesus Christ is relationships. Relationship with God and relationships with humankind. It's really that simple. Having relationships with all people and being inclusive is winning. Building walls of any kind or banning others from inclusion is losing. At least according to God.

Let's examine that *relational* concept for a moment. In my book *Demystifying the Cue* (a book about writing music for film and TV) I proposed to my readers that they seek to embrace the great importance and value of "networking" (which I defined simply as *having relationships* with people in the music business) through studying some well-known ancient writings. These writings are the ones we commonly refer to as "The Ten Commandments." I wanted to show the musicians, songwriters, composers and music producers that even the traditional, Judeo-Christian God put the utmost emphasis on relationships.

I've modified what I wrote in *Demystifying the Cue* and made it appropriate for this book. (I think it's reasonable to assume that most of you are not pursuing a career in Film and TV music and would not otherwise check out that book. If you have read it, consider this a refresher.)

The Ten Commandments (Relationships)

Let's take a look at these Ten Commandments said to have been etched in stone so many years ago and see if they support the idea of banning, excluding and walling off people, or if they support a more inclusive philosophy. OK? Stay with me. Here we go.

1. *I am the Lord thy God. You shall have no other Gods before me.* This is pretty clear. God is proclaiming to be THEE Big Kahuna. I think it also means we should put God first and foremost in our lives, spending time with God in an ongoing *relationship*.

2. *Don't make up your own "gods."*
Stop worshiping money or success or your own opinions the way Dean Krippaehne sometimes does. Also, this commandment directs us again to value our *relationship* with God.

3. *Don't take the name of God in vain.*
Bam! Value and respect the *relationship* you have with God – don't crap on it. A lot of people think this commandment means "don't swear." It probably does to some degree, but I tend to think

31

it means something far greater. We can dump on God's name just by refusing to love and care for those around us. This is certainly much more destructive than simply blurting out "goddammit" when a hammer hits our thumb. Whatever the intended meaning behind this commandment, a *relationship* with God, honoring and respecting God by loving others, is at its core.

4. *Keep Holy the Sabbath.*
This commandment may be pointing to a particular day or an amount of time each week to keep "holy." Keeping a day or a certain amount of time *holy* each week means setting aside the concerns of our life and spending that day or daily time with God. The main point is to spend your "Sabbath" time in *relationship* with God, in your heart, in your mind, and with those around you. It is also God wanting to have a *relationship* with us as we rest, reflect, rejuvenate and replenish our personal well of health and love.

5. *Honor your father and mother.*
This *doesn't* mean our parents are (or were) always right. It means we should strive as best we can to have a respectful, caring *relationship* with our parents.

6. *Thou shalt not murder.*
Don't murder anyone. Human life is valuable. Always be healthy enough in your *relationships* so you don't become so angry or hateful or fearful that you began to consider violence or murder as an option. Also be aware that murder is not simply bound to the physical. It is possible to "murder" or harm someone physically, emotionally, psychologically or spiritually.

7. *Do not commit adultery.*
Don't screw someone who is married (or while you are married) or you will screw up your *relationships*.

8. *Thou shalt not steal.*
Other people's stuff is other people's stuff, not yours. Keep your *relationships* with everyone respectful.

9. *Thou shalt not bear false witness.*
Don't be a liar. You want to keep honesty central in all your *relationships*.

10. *Don't covet thy neighbor's wife or goods, or anything else.*
She (or he) may be hot, but you need to respect and honor them and their spouse (and their stuff) enough to keep your *relationships* pure.

Do you see it - the word *relationship*? Amazing, isn't it? Each one of these Ten Commandments is about *relationships* with others and with God. God really has a theme going on here. Without ever even reading the rest of the Bible, I think we can ascertain that *relationships* were and are of the utmost importance to God.

God values people. All people.

Got it?

Good.

Yoga and the Scrambled Eggs

Not too long ago, I woke up to one of those peaceful, perfect mornings. You know the kind. My kids were off to school and my wife had left early to go to work. I was working from home that day and had the peace and quiet of the house all to myself. Just me and my dog, a little Sheltie named Yoga, left alone to take in the lazy calm of a brand new day.

It almost felt like a vacation. Like freedom. It was *my* morning and I was going to make the most of it.

I started by treating myself to a nice hot breakfast of old fashioned oatmeal with lots of brown sugar and raisins on it. I also found some honey baked ham in the fridge and decided that cooking it with some scrambled eggs would make a wonderful addition to my feast. I put on a pot of French Roast coffee and actually took the time to squeeze my own fresh orange juice.

It was perfect.

I thought as long as I was the only one home I would take my meal into the living room, usually a forbidden eating venue, sit on the comfy couch, and feast away while watching the morning TV shows.

So there I was, sitting on the couch with my steaming bowl of oatmeal and my hot plate of ham and eggs on the coffee table, ready to experience my leisurely bliss.

Just as I was about to take my first bite, I heard my cell phone buzzing in the other room. I sighed and got up to answer it. It was my wife. She had forgotten something and wanted me to bring it to her at work. "No problem," I said, "I'll have it there in about an hour."

I walked back into the living room to enjoy my breakfast feast, but something was wrong. I hadn't even been out of the room for one minute, and yet my steaming hot, mouth-watering plate of ham and eggs was entirely gone. Well, my plate was still there, but the delicious meal was nowhere in sight. All that was left was the lingering aroma.

I looked down at my dog, Yoga. He was licking his chops and seemed to have a satisfied though slightly guilty smile on his face. Yup. Yoga had devoured the entire plate of ham and eggs in less than one minute. I looked at him and yelled, "YOGA!!! Bad Dog!" He hung his head and cowered over to the other side of the room.

The temptation had just been too great for him. The sight and smell of those eggs and that ham in such close proximity was simply overwhelming. Pretty soon he walked over to me, cautiously wagging his tail with an "I'm sorry" look on his face. I reached down and petted him and said "it's OK." He happily wagged his tail and then laid down next to my feet by the couch.

About ten minutes later he threw up all over the living room carpet.

Yuck!

Isn't that the way it sometimes goes in our lives? We are tempted by something that really seems appealing to us and even though we know it is bad or wrong we do it anyway. Inevitably, we pay the price.

Being tempted by power, prestige and political gain that prompts one to travel down the path of exclusion can only lead to suffering. To those who have already headed down this road I can only hope that you will find your way back.

Indeed, I am tremendously dismayed that many non-Christians around the world have come to believe that this "exclusion of *other*" theology practiced by some in the Evangelical community - this denying of a place at the table of Jesus - is the way all Christians think and behave. That we condone the banning of entire groups of people from anything. We don't.

What grieves me the most, however, is that some of these non-believers - because they have received the message that Christians exclude - may have sworn off getting to know Jesus, forever.

Racism, Hate and Exclusion of Other

I'm pretty sure Jesus wasn't a racist.

Let me rephrase that.

Jesus wasn't a racist.

I mean, He welcomed and loved all people. Let me say that again: He welcomed *all people* to come to His table, to come and follow him, to enter into His Kingdom. All people. He didn't say only some people from certain countries were welcome. Nor did He say only people who look a certain way were welcome. He didn't even say you had to belong to a particular religion or have a certain sexual identity to be welcome. Nope. Jesus welcomed all people. ALL people. He welcomed the sinners and tax collectors, the prostitutes and adulterers, the poor and the sick, the healthy and the rich. He didn't care if you were young or old. If you wanted to follow Him, you were welcomed.

Indeed, Jesus welcomes all people to come into his fold. This is indisputable in ancient scripture.

On the other side of the coin we have a politician holding the highest office in the land saying things like, *"go back"* [to where you came from - paraphrased] to a United States Congresswoman of color. This phrase is a well-known racist trope in the United States. Appallingly, because of that politician's racist words, thousands of his supporters chanted the very same racist trope, *send her back,** in unison at one of his campaign rallies. Additionally, many of his supporters began sharing it on social media, spreading this racist hate to millions.

We have thousands more people who claim to be followers of Christ yet are saying there is nothing wrong with this racist chant. Tragically, there are Christians who are supporting this racism and its propagators wholeheartedly. Still other Christians are deafening in their silence of not condemning this blatant bigotry.

The unfortunate reality is that Christians who are supporting or engaging in this kind of racist language are not only hurting those on the receiving end of these tropes and fueling the fires of hate in this country, but they are also sending a message to the world that Jesus is racist. Since Jesus is emphatically not a racist, this behavior can only be described as anti-Jesus.

Jesus said, *"let the little children come to me"* (Matthew 19:14,) and, *anyone who keeps these children from coming to me it would be better that he or she tied a rock to their foot and cast themselves into the deep waters (Luke 7:2 paraphrased).* Since we are all God's children you can be absolutely certain that Jesus doesn't like the phrase, "send her back."

* *"Send her back"* https://www.washingtonpost.com/powerpost/omar-trump-rally-with-send-her-back-chant-will-be-defining-moment-in-us-history/2019/07/25/acada110-aecd-11e9-bc5c-e73b603e7f38_story.html

Therefore, Christians who are supporting or engaging in this or any type of racist language or behavior are quite possibly keeping the children of the world from coming to Jesus. Let me repeat the essence of what Jesus said about this: *anyone who keeps these children from coming to me it would be better that he or she tied a rock to their foot and cast themselves into the deep waters.*

We are all God's children. Jesus welcomes *ALL PEOPLE.*

Period. Yet...

There have been politicians who wave the Christian banner supporting neo-Nazis. A particular case in Charlottesville, Virginia, involving white supremacists at a Unite the Right rally was utterly disturbing. It was a rally of White Supremacists and Neo-Nazis marching and engaging in racist chants including: *"Jews will not replace us! You will not replace us!"* and *"blood and soil."** Let's be perfectly clear. Nazis are racists. Neo-Nazis are racist. White Supremacists are racist. The lion's share of their philosophy is built upon a foundation of racism and the exclusion of "other." They believe white people to be somehow a supreme race of people. Supporting these neo-Nazis in Charlottesville (or anywhere) or equating them to genuine protesters is, in fact, supporting racism.

Again, Jesus was not and is not racist.

As followers of Christ we must speak loudly and boldly against racist statements and actions. We cannot sit idly by and remain quiet. Jesus loves all people. Jesus condemns hate. Christians must let this be known. We must shout it from the rooftops lest we be guilty of driving another nail into His cross.

* Neo Nazi and White Supremacists chant "Blood and soil" and other chants at a Unite the Right rally in Charlottesville, Virginia.
https://abcnews.go.com/US/happen-charlottesville-protest-anniversary-weekend/story?id=57107500

Some conservative, white Evangelicals, however, have remained utterly silent while the politicians they support have made false equivalences between racists and those who protest against hate. This boggles the mind.

Also, dehumanizing any people or using dehumanizing vernacular which contributes to an exclusionary philosophy is not something Jesus would ever do. It is completely contrary to His nature. For us to support or engage in this type of language is not Christ Kingdom-building. It is Christ-Kingdom-destroying. And labeling a group of people in a dehumanizing way - people who are fleeing their dangerous homelands in search of asylum, in search of a better life for their children, who are poor, tired and hungry - is anti-Jesus.

Donald Trump has called asylum-seeking immigrants and refugees at the Mexican border among other things: "drug dealers," "criminals," "rapists," "very bad people," and "an invasion."

Defining any particular group of people as rapist and murderers, gangs and thugs, or saying that they are "infesting" our country is certainly dehumanizing vernacular. History teaches us that this type of dehumanizing language from a country's leadership will hasten the evil process of segregating groups of people, treating them inhumanly, and eventually lead to the torturing, killing or exterminating of innocents.

We need to be clear that Christ welcomes all people.

Let us always seek to call out racist language and racist actions when we hear or see them. Let us be quick to identify and quick to condemn that type of vitriol. Let us always strive to build bridges of love and understanding between all types of people instead of constructing walls of segregation and destruction. Our God is a God of welcoming, a God of relationships and a God who loves and cares deeply for everyone. Let us follow God's great example in that way and in every way.

White Nationalism and White Entitlement

There has always been a strong undercurrent of racism ever-flowing toward its goal of White Nationalism in various racist groups and among many political, business and religious organizations in this country. This is the undeniable reality of the history of the United States. However, there is something much more subtle that also needs addressing. Something that many of my white friends don't believe exists. That is:

The great denial among white people in the United States about the reality of "white entitlement."

Please note that I'm not talking about blatant racists when I speak of white entitlement. I'm not even talking about racist-adjacent people. I'm talking about white people who have led lives of integrity trying their best to treat all people equally but who, at least in part, *because* of this ethical life they have led, don't see themselves as having any special privileges because they happen to be white. My only response to this is - *you don't see it because you haven't yet looked deeply enough.*

All of us white people living in the United States have been infected in one way or another by the historical and systemic epidemic of hate and ignorance when it comes to the issue of race. It is ingrained within our culture and we must continually look in the mirror of self-examination searching our minds and souls to identify and root out our misbeliefs about this issue, disputing them with the truth.

We must do the same by looking objectively at our society and such things as economic privilege, the generational accumulation of wealth, redlining, incarceration, and racial disparity in the criminal justice system. We must question things as simple as why Dean Krippaehne (a white man) can jay-walk without ever thinking about getting ticketed while Dean's black friends must always wonder if jay-walking will get them a ticket - or worse.

If white people can develop a lifelong habit of educating themselves to the realities of white entitlement they can become healthier individuals and play a more active role in growing a much healthier and equitable society.

Let honest reflection, truth and love rule.

I have been in certain small towns in the southern part of the United States where it is still, culturally speaking, very much like the 1950's in many ways. While the laws may have changed, the attitudes of many have not. I have also been a firsthand witness to the manifestation of systemic racism in Seattle (where I live). This disappoints me greatly. One of the challenges in a relatively progressive city like Seattle is that many white people I run across, young and old, don't think there's much of a problem here. Sadly, there is.

The good news is that all of us are capable of change. Through education, self-awareness, identifying our cognitive distortions and committing ourselves to a lifelong pursuit of gaining the perspective of others, we can transform our minds. By fostering inclusiveness and loving our neighbors we can begin to turn the tide, remembering that everyone is our neighbor and that love is an actionable - not just a feeling or emotion.

*"So in everything, **do** to others what you would have them do to you." - Jesus (Matthew 7:12)*

There is nothing much more illuminating (and cringe worthy) than hearing a bunch of white people discussing what life is like for a person of color in this country. If we white-entitled people are honest with ourselves we must admit that we have little to no idea what it is like to live as a person of color in the United States of America. Once we have come to that fundamental realization we can begin to listen with open ears, minds and hearts to those who actually navigate these issues on a daily basis.

A revolution of unity is possible if only we will *make* the time to listen and understand.

LGBTQ

Really?

Are ya gonna make me go there?

Have not we yet learned Jesus' great lesson of inclusivity?

Do not we yet understand the exclusion of *other* is anti-Jesus?

OK then... Let me say this once and let me say it loudly so that everyone can hear. Jesus welcomes all people to his table. *All people*. Did you hear me? ALL PEOPLE.

Christians saying otherwise are wrong.

As I've stated before, Jesus didn't say He only welcomes some people. He didn't say only people who have purple skin and bow ties can be His followers. Nor did He say only people who have red hair with white streaks are welcome at His table. Jesus is all inclusive. His Kingdom isn't just for chubby people, or skinny people, or academics, or the illiterate, or straight, or gay or any other kind of people. Jesus does not exclude. Jesus welcomes us all.

An exclusion of any type of people is *not of Jesus* and implying that exclusion of other is somehow of Jesus Christ is a hijacking of Christianity.

There is not a lot more I can say on this. But if one does not understand that the love of Jesus is all inclusive then I question whether one really knows the heart of Christ at all.

Also, cherry-picking Bible passages for the purpose of backing up one's own agenda is bad theology. Any passage in the Bible interpreted in such a way that does not fit with the Bible as a whole is a dangerous and faulty interpretation.

Cherry Picking Snakes

I know a guy who grew up in a small town in Kentucky. In that town was a tiny Christian church. This church had cherry-picked the Bible and made one particular Bible phrase, *"they will pick up snakes with their hands; ...and it will not hurt them at all" (Mark 16:18)*, a pillar of their theology. When you walked into this little Kentucky church you could see pictures on the wall of all the parishioners who had died from handling poisonous snakes in that church.

My friends, the handling of poisonous snakes as a test of faith is goofy nonsense! This practice got people killed. Cherry-picking any Biblical phrase to justify an agenda or an action can be quite dangerous. This is why all of the Biblical passages I have used in this book to underscore various points are either repeated multiple times throughout the Bible (used in the same context as the stories they were drawn from) or they are in unity with the Bible as a whole.

The way you hear some conservative Evangelicals cherry-picking and weaponizing scriptural quotes you would think that instead of *revealing* Jesus through the Bible they are instead *replacing* Jesus with the Bible.

The cherry-picking and weaponizing of Biblical scripture has sadly happened in abundance with reference to the LGBTQ community. There has been a historical epidemic of people pulling one or two phrases out of the Bible and using them in such a way that precludes the overriding Biblical theme that God loves us all equally. *"For God so loved the world." (John 3:16)* So many people have been wounded, killed and murdered because of cherry-picking Christians. It is one of the main reasons I wrote this book.

Often the opponents of LGBTQ, those throwing stones, will cherry-pick the Bible for verses that they claim support their position. They will cite a couple of Old Testament phrases or one or two lines the Apostle Paul wrote in ancient Biblical scripture to make their case. As I have previously stated, I call this weaponizing the Bible. What they usually fail to bring forth is the fact that the very same Paul they are citing to support their anti-LGTBQ agenda also gives a beautiful description of love in Corinthians and doesn't mention sexual preference or gender identity at all.

"Love is patient, love is kind. It does not envy, it does not boast. It is not proud. It does not dishonor others, it is not self-seeking, it is not easily angered, it keeps no record of wrongs." (1 Corinthians 13: 4-5)

What Paul talks about is love of the heart, love in being Christ-like, love of being healthy mentally and healthy spiritually. People are not excluded from this message based on their sexuality or gender identity. Similarly, when Jesus says, *"love your neighbor as yourself"* He doesn't put a qualifier in His message. He doesn't say "love your neighbor as yourself, unless they are LGBTQ."

Context matters.

The whole of Jesus's teaching is concerned with the state of our heart. Not the state of our dinner choices, our car purchases, or our sexual preference. Got it?

The Piano Gig

In 1991, I had a house piano gig at a club on the shores of Lake Union in Seattle. One Friday night each month a group of seven or eight guys, all in their thirties and forties, would come in and sit around the piano, requesting songs and singing along with their favorites. It was a blast watching them enjoy the music we all made together.

As the months passed by, one of the guys started looking quite ill. A few months later another one became increasingly ill. By the end of the year, four of these men were no longer looking healthy at all yet they continued to come in and sing, each of the healthy ones helping the increasingly weakened (and dying) others. I don't think I've ever seen a greater display of love for one another in my life. The way these men took care of each other in their hour of desperate need most certainly is the greatest love of all.

This monthly hang-out continued through 1992 but by the end of that year only five of these friends were able to make it in to sing with me. Others began to get ill. By the end of 1993, only one was left. All the rest had died.

What I wouldn't give to have one more night of singing along with their smiling faces.

AIDS is an insidious disease.

A friend of mine recently posted a video online of Freddie Mercury, former singer in the band Queen. It was the last video this artist would ever make. It made me remember these wonderful guys around the piano who brought so much joy into my life, who took such great care of one another under the most dire of circumstances - and who taught me so very much about what love really is.

I miss them.

Yes. They all happened to be gay. That didn't matter. It doesn't matter.

Please, Christians, stop hijacking Jesus's definition of love to serve your own opinions.

Less Than

"So God created mankind in his own image, in the image of God he created them; male and female he created them." (Genesis 1:27) All people were created in God's image, not just some people.

No human born on this planet is, in God's eyes, less than any other. Not a person from a foreign country, nor a person of a different color, nor a person with a different religion, and not a person with a different sexual preference or gender identity than yours. No one is *less than* in God's eyes. Any mention or notion to the contrary is not of the Almighty God who created the Universe but rather has its roots in some personal opinion, or some screwy Biblical interpretation, or political agenda.

We're all the same and beautiful in God's eyes and God loves us all unconditionally and equally. It is way past time to stop bashing people just because they are not like you or they don't fit into your vision of what you think humanity should be. Jesus is not cool with that. He doesn't dig this kind of judgmental stone throwing.

When any belief system harms other people or makes someone feel *less than*, that system has walked away from the God of Christianity. It is merely an opinion of a person who is part of a fallen humanity. We can all have our own unique belief systems and opinions but for God's sake (literally) we must stop hurting people who are not like us.

God loves us all.

Amen.

Words Matter

These are the Words of Jesus:

"Love your neighbor"

"Feed my sheep"

"Care for the widows and the orphans"

"All are welcome"

"Whatever you do to the least of these you do to me"

"When you give a banquet, invite the poor, the crippled, the lame, the blind"

There are many people today using deception as a weapon, twisting facts and distorting the Word of God to move forward their own personal, political or religious agenda. Let's look back at some ancient scripture and let the power of its wisdom soak into our minds and hearts for a moment.

"Rather, we have renounced secret and shameful ways; we do not use deception, nor do we distort the word of God. On the contrary, by setting forth the truth plainly we commend ourselves to everyone's conscience in the sight of God." (2 Corinthians 4:2)

The Apostle Paul wrote these words in a letter to the Corinthians nearly 2000 years ago. They are still as strong, relevant and drastically needed today as we witness flawed humans continuing to deceive others by distorting God's Word.

A Troubling Trend

It has been said that dehumanization leads to ghettoization leads to extermination. There's horrific proof of this in the rise of the Third Reich in the 1930s. Alarmingly, there has been a growing amount of dehumanizing rhetoric in the United States being used against certain peoples. This language is especially prevalent in the comments and tweets made by President Donald Trump who has used the following language when referring to non-white people:

"Shit-hole Countries," "Rapists and Murderers," "Sick and diseased" "a Rat and Rodent infested mess," "These aren't people" "These are animals."

Yes, these are all actual comments made by the President of the United States.

Let that sink in for a minute.

If we learn nothing else from our past let us remember that the dehumanization rhetoric of the 1930s in Germany lead to the ghettoization of the Jewish people, which paved way for the systematic extermination of our fellow human beings.

Any dehumanizing rhetoric or segregation of a particular group of people needs to be recognized, called out and immediately stopped in its tracks - otherwise extermination becomes an inevitability. Does this seem far-fetched? Read a history book.

Christians and Christian leaders who support politicians who make vitriolic comments like these need to loudly and with no reservation call out this disturbing type of rhetoric when they hear it.

Sadly, many have remained silent.

February, 2018

In a New York Times article published early in 2018, Rev. Franklin Graham, one of America's most recognized Evangelical Christian leaders said this:

> *"People say that the president says mean things. I can't think of anything mean he's said. I think he speaks what he feels," "I think he's trying to speak the truth."*

I'll also let that one sink in for a bit.

Prior to that statement, Donald Trump had said the following about various people: *"Dumb as a rock" "Mental Basketcase" "Grab them by the pussy" "desperate" "choker" "a nasty guy" "I moved on her like a bitch" "a loser" "sleazebag" "Angry, Dumb and Sick" "comes off as a crazed & stumbling lunatic."*

Yeah.

Rev. Franklin Graham and I must have a vastly different definition of what is *mean* and what is truthful.

When Trump has described various women as *"a dog," "a pig," "horseface,"* as well as *"bleeding badly from a facelift"* and having *"blood coming out of her wherever."* The response by many Evangelical Christian leaders to this highly rude and disrespectful language has been positively lame. It blows my mind just how lame their responses have been.

While most Trump-supporting Christians and Evangelical Christian leaders haven't condoned this type of language, many have responded to it by saying, "I wouldn't have used those words" or something to that effect. That is weak. Really weak. It sends the message to non-Christians at home and abroad that Christians in the United States are OK with their Commander-in-Chief belittling and making derogatory statements about a woman's appearance or demeanor.

It also sends the message that Jesus is OK with belittling people.

When Jesus said, *"Sell all that you have... ...and then come, follow me" (Matthew 19:21),* He wasn't just talking about material possessions, He was also referring to our inner life. Sell all the lust you have for power and prestige and then come follow me. Sell all of your opinions and then come follow me. Sell your right to do as you please and then come follow me. Sell even what you *think you know* about God and then come follow me. Put your political agenda aside and come follow me.

And again Jesus said, *"If any want to become my followers, let them deny themselves and take up their cross daily and follow me. (Luke 9:23)* Put aside your desires, your convenience, your comfort, your privilege, your right to yourself, and *humbly* walk with me.

I know Jesus was talking to me too in these passages because at times I find myself holding on to my opinions and bias as if they were mini gods themselves. My guess is the He is also appealing to Rev. Franklin Graham and others with these words right now. *"Sell all that you have... [Franklin Graham] ...and then come, follow me."*

Polar Ice Caps in the Bible?

It was appalling to me on multiple levels to hear pastor and Presidential advisor Robert Jeffress's comments in response to sixteen year old Greta Thunberg's climate activism:

"Somebody needs to read poor Greta Genesis, Chapter 9," Jeffress said, *"and tell her the next time she worries about global warming, just look at a rainbow. That's God's promise that the polar ice caps aren't going to melt and flood the world again."*

Let us take a moment and refresh our memories to this line in Genesis 9 that Robert Jeffress was most likely referring to.

[God said to Noah] *"I establish my covenant with you: Never again will all life be destroyed by the waters of a flood; never again will there be a flood to destroy the earth." (Genesis 9:11)*

I find it somewhat baffling that Robert Jeffress feels the need to respond to sixteen year old Greta Thunberg simply because her climate activism differs from the climate agenda he supports. Why is he so fearful of her? Robert Jeffress also needs to re-read Genesis 9 because his comment is not at all what it says nor what it means. Let me first state the obvious: God was not talking about *polar ice caps* thousands of years ago in the Bible no matter what translation of ancient Hebrew one believes to be accurate.

Furthermore, even if you take Genesis 9 as literal, God didn't say he *wouldn't* send a flood to destroy *some* of the earth or *some* life. Like a few billion people or so. Nope. God said to Noah he wouldn't destroy *all* life nor *all* the world. God's covenant in this passage - in keeping with the Bible as a whole - probably has much more to do with this: as God saved Noah from the flood with the Ark, so too God saved humanity from the flood of sin through the death and resurrection of Jesus Christ. Robert Jeffress, in addition to his misinterpretation of Genesis, seems to be cherry-picking the Bible to support his own political opinion. This is a hijacking of Christianity. Robert Jeffress is an educated man who I'm sure loves the Lord, but he should know better than to use the Bible in such a twisted manner. He is supposed to be representing Jesus. Not the President. Not his opinion on climate change. And he should not be twisting scripture to advance his own political beliefs or personal prestige.

Back to Trump's belittling rhetoric.

I want to take just a moment to assure any non-Christians reading these pages that most of us who are followers of and believers in Jesus Christ *do not condone in any way* the rude belittlement, disparaging behavior or misleading falsehoods of our commander in chief, Donald Trump, nor do we agree with certain Christian Leaders who seemingly have no problem with Trump's behaviors.

We strongly, forcefully and with one voice condemn behavior that harms or misleads people this way or in any way. Just as Jesus does.

Words, Actions and Hypocrisy

A question for Christians.

Are you using Jesus for your own purpose or are you being used by Jesus for His great purpose?

Hopefully, it's the latter.

Most certainly both major political parties have used their interpretation of Jesus or His teachings to advance an agenda at times. In recent years the Democrats have often leaned on Jesus to justify their use of government resources for feeding the hungry, taking care of the poor and sick, etc., while the Republicans have used God for purposes such as promoting their anti-abortion or anti-LGBTQ positions. Additionally, both parties have endorsed the use of military force on moral (Christian) grounds at one time or another.

While both parties in the United States have used the Bible of Christianity in these ways from time to time, I don't think I have ever witnessed such blatant disregard for many of Christ's teachings as I have seen coming from the white Evangelical Christian supporters of the Trump administration. The hypocrisy is astonishing. Because of it I have been referring to myself as "a follower of Jesus" rather than as a Christian. This is simply because the label "Christian" has been so besmirched by the Evangelical-right's hypocrisy and political agenda it has become more of a road block rather than a welcoming bridge when addressing myself to non-Christians.

The un-labeling of myself as a Christian is not something I want to do. As a follower of and believer in Jesus I am, indeed, technically a Christian. And in the past I have liked calling myself a Christian. But these days, as soon as I identify myself as a Christian to non-believers or to people of other faiths, walls go up, doors get locked, opinions have already been formulated and I'm immediately branded as one of "them." The intolerant. The non-inclusive. The judgmental.

The relabeling of Christians from caring servants to intolerant political hacks has undermined the building of the communication bridges that Jesus so desired for His disciples. It is also killing the chance some will ever get to hear the words of Jesus.

It has long been known that the number one thing that keeps people from coming to Christ is Christians. I sense, too, that this sad state of affairs has been greatly heightened in the Age of Trump. With all the crazy talk and hypocrisy of a few well known Evangelical leaders, who can blame any non-Christian if they turn and head for the hills? The total disregard for holding accountable the integrity, character and common decency of Donald Trump (and turning a blind eye to what conservative Christians used to profess as immorality) has, I fear, caused many more to forgo a

Dean Krippaehne

relationship with Jesus.

In other words, Christianity has been hijacked by those with either bad theology or ulterior personal or political motives.

Words matter. Actions matter. Character matters. When Christian leaders fail to call out the words and actions of the politicians they support who continually falter in these virtues, vast numbers of potential Christ followers turn away from the church. This grieves me greatly.

Are you OK with that?

I have a few questions for the Evangelicals and other Christians still strongly supporting Donald Trump as some kind of savior for Christianity but who are remaining silent about his visceral, verbal attacks on individuals and other indiscretions. But before I start, remember that responding with "those are not words I would have chosen" is a weak cop-out.

Here goes:

When Donald Trump insulted Jeff Bezos by calling him "Jeff Bozo" or calling Mika Brzezinski "dumb as a rock," or insulted TV host Don Lemon calling him "the dumbest man on television" or when he continually refers to U.S. Senator Elizabeth Warren as "Pocahontas" - Are you OK with that?

When Donald Trump calls neo-Nazis and white supremacists "very fine people" - Are you OK with that?

When Donald Trump (referring to women) said that as a star he could just "grab 'em by the pussy" - Are you OK with that?

When Donald Trump had an extramarital affair with a porn star - were you OK with that?

When Donald Trump allegedly directed his attorney to pay hush money to keep his affairs with both a porn star and a Playboy model quiet - were you OK with that?

When Donald Trump told four congresswomen of color to go back to where they came from (a well-known racist trope) and allowed the crowd at one of his rallies to chant, "send her back" - Are you OK with that?

When Donald Trump continues with his incessant lying - are you OK with that?

When Donald Trump and his administration separate parents from little children, putting some of them in cages and not allowing them proper medical treatment - Are you OK with that?

When Donald Trump called for banning certain people from entering the United States because of their religion - were you OK with that?

When Donald Trump continually brags and boasts and calls himself "the chosen one" while looking up towards the heavens - Are you OK with that?

Are you OK with these things?

Jesus isn't.

It was Jesus who said, "...*But the things that come out of a person's mouth come from the heart, and these defile them.*" *(Matthew 15:18)*

So again, I ask all you Evangelical supporters of Donald Trump, why do you remain silent on these issues?

Are you not *using* Christianity to promote your favorite politician?

This is the *hijacking of Christianity.*

People are watching.

Non-Christians are listening to you - and listening for your voice.

People who may have been curious about Jesus are watching - and sadly turning away.

If any Christian Trump supporters are still reading and haven't yet burned this book, please re-read the above section, only this time insert either the name Hillary Clinton or Barack Obama. Or maybe insert your child's name where the name Donald Trump is.

Now tell me how you feel.

Do Words Have Consequences?

On Saturday night, August 3rd, 2019, after traveling over 600 miles to a Walmart in El Paso, Texas, a gunman* with an agenda took the lives of 22 people and wounded 24 more. Before this massacre the shooter released a manifesto with white nationalist themes and cited the "Hispanic invasion of Texas" as one of the reasons for his deranged, terrorist actions.

One of the more troubling aspects with part of the shooter's motive was that it seemed to directly mirror the assertions of Donald Trump. In the months preceding the shooting, Donald Trump had made the following disparaging and dehumanizing claims against the immigrants attempting to enter the United States via the Mexican border.

"We cannot allow all of these people to *invade* our Country,"

"As everyone knows, the United States of America has been *invaded* by hundreds of thousands of people coming through Mexico and entering our country illegally."

* El Paso shooting and gunman's manifesto.
https://www.usatoday.com/story/news/nation/2019/08/05/dayton-ohio-el-paso-shootings-weekend-mass-killings-2019/1919633001/
* Donald Trump's use of the term "invasion."

https://www.nbcnews.com/think/opinion/trump-s-anti-immigrant-invasion-rhetoric-was-echoed-el-paso-ncna1039286

"We're talking about an *invasion* of our country with drugs, with human traffickers, with all types of criminals and gangs."

"At this very moment, large, well-organized caravans of migrants are marching towards our southern border. Some people call it an '*invasion*.' It's like an *invasion*. They have violently overrun the Mexican border."

In addition, Donald Trump had also publicly referred to White Nationalists as "very fine people."

Although one cannot directly link this El Paso atrocity to Donald Trump, it is not a far stretch to think that the shooter was most likely influenced by his inflammatory language.

We must be clear. Donald Trump did *not* actually make this terrorist pick up a gun and kill people.

But...

Do words matter?

Yes.

And as President Donald Trump made his disturbing claims against immigrants along with his "very fine people" statement about White Nationalists, some of his conservative Evangelical supporters remained deafeningly silent.

Hijack.

The Need for Speed

Have you ever gone really fast in your car on the freeway?

Have you ever gone sixty-five or seventy-five miles per hour on the freeway?

OK, another question. Have you ever gone eighty-five or ninety miles per hour on the freeway? If you have ever gone that fast, do you remember the feeling? Oh yeah baby! And if you crank it up to ninety-five it's even more intense.

How about this: Have you ever gone eighty miles-per-hour on a motorcycle? Not that I've ever done that, but going eighty mph on a motorcycle *feels* a lot faster than going eighty miles an hour in a car.

What about me? Alright, I'll fess up. The fastest I've ever gone on the freeway was one-hundred-and-five miles per hour when I was a teenager. It was awesome! It was also stupid, dangerous, against the law, and I regret that I put other's lives in danger by being that foolish.

That sensation of speed is really something, isn't it?

It's something we can feel and we can sense and we can experience.

It is tangible.

Now I'm going to ask you a question that may seem a little bit weird. Wherever you are sitting (or laying or standing) right now, does it feel the same as going ninety miles per hour in a car? (Hopefully you're not reading this while going ninety mph in a car) I will assume for the sake of this illustration that you are sitting somewhere other than in a moving vehicle. Can you feel the wind in your face when you are sitting in your chair? Nope. Not unless you are sitting outside on a windy day. Can you feel the rattle of the vehicle and sensation of speed along with that combination of fear and excitement as you sit there sipping on your cup of coffee? No. Of course not. You can't feel anything of the sort while sitting still.

Now I'm going to tell you something that will blow your mind.

Did you know that as you are sitting there and I'm sitting here - we are traveling at a speed of one-thousand miles per hour? It's true. The Earth's rotation speed is right around one-thousand miles per hour. Buckle up!

It's weird, isn't it? We're all traveling faster than most of us have ever traveled, save maybe an astronaut or a fighter pilot, yet *we can't feel a thing*. We can't see it, we can't touch it, we can't smell it, and yet it's true. We are indeed going one-thousand miles per hour right now!

Some things we can see and feel. And we know they are true.

Other things we cannot see nor feel - yet they are still true.

Why do I tell you this?

Because we live in a time where certain leaders in our nation are continually making misleading statements. They are continually tweeting falsehoods, lying, bullying and calling respected leaders silly schoolyard names. They are talking in rude and unkind ways, regularly belittling people as well as using racist tropes and other dehumanizing language.

This derogatory language is having an effect. A negative effect. An eroding effect. We may not be able to see the effect in real time, just as we cannot see or feel ourselves traveling at one thousand miles per hour, but that doesn't disprove the reality of what is happening.

Maybe even worse, this behavior is becoming normalized. Today there are literally thousands of instances of this type of corrosive language circulating throughout our greater media-sphere. What used to shock us barely even gets a roll of the eyes anymore. And what about our children? Indeed, they are learning that it is OK to bully. They are learning to belittle and that it's OK to call people names. They are soaking up the idea that bad behavior has no consequence and lying is acceptable.

It's crazy.

Yup, the chairs you and I are sitting in right now are affixed to a world that is spinning at the speed of one thousand miles per hour and we don't even feel it. But it is happening. It is real.

So, too, is the reality that the erosion of common decency and the demise of integrity in our society is infecting our children. We may not be able to measure it in a tangible way yet... but we will.

And, as evidenced by their remaining silent instead of calling out this bad behavior, a few Christian leaders and their congregations are perfectly OK with this.

Another hijack.

I Want to be Just Like You

So, I'm driving my car down a four lane road near the town of Puyallup, Washington. I've got my three year old daughter Crystal, in the passenger seat (a car seat) next to me. We are having a good father-daughter time singing silly little songs when all of a sudden a car swerves into my lane almost clipping the front end of my car. They obviously didn't look and didn't see me at all.

My reaction was to immediately swerve my own vehicle in an attempt to avoid a collision. That's when the real bad stuff happened. Did I get into an accident? No. Thank God. But what did occur was almost as bad. Not really, but almost.

After avoiding the collision I launched into an adolescent tirade. I let out a string of cuss words that would make a truck driver blush. I was ticked off! The distracted driver could have killed my daughter. And although it happened quite fast, I think that there might have been a hand gesture involved - by me.

To make matters worse, when I looked over at my three year old, innocent daughter, instead of saying "I'm sorry" to her, I said something else. I looked right at her and said, "Don't tell mommy I said those words."

It wasn't one of my more stellar moments as a dad.

Let's take a pause here and recap what I have just taught my daughter. First, I have taught her that when someone does something that you don't like, you are to GET VERY ANGRY AND EXPLODE. Secondly, I have shown her that when you do explode there are some highly inappropriate words and a hand gesture you can use to punctuate your anger. And finally I've taught her the most important thing any child should know: When you do something wrong you should lie to your mother.

Why do I tell you this? Not to bash myself for poor parenting, but to illustrate that words *do* matter, actions *do* matter and what we as adults do, our children will soak up and imitate.

When we and our children hear things over and over again, things that Donald Trump has said (and keeps repeating), like *"Dumb as a rock" "Mental Basketcase" "Grab them by the pussy" "choker" "a nasty guy" "I moved on her like a bitch" "fake news" "a loser" "sleazebag" "Angry, Dumb and Sick,"* our children will sponge those attitudes and that language right up. They will begin to integrate this into their vernacular and thought process because *that's what children do.* They imitate and emulate us. Thanks to the behavior of our country's leaders, our children will learn that it's OK to use insulting phrases in a derogatory way towards others. Thus begins a new institutional level of societal degradation.

In much the same way, when Christians and Christian leaders support the ones continually making these undignified remarks without calling them out, their support adds power to the normalization of such behavior. Their condoning of this conduct begins to infiltrate both our individual and collective character, leading us to a lower standard for human kindness. A race to the bottom. And Jesus Christ is wounded deeply.

Absurdities

Here's an absurd statement from former White House press secretary, Sarah Sanders:

> *"I think God calls all of us to fill different roles at different times and **I think that He wanted Donald Trump to become president.**"**

Here's another:

> *"We have guns because it's our God-given right enshrined in the Constitution."*

Both of the above statements by Sarah Sanders are absurd. Did God really want Donald Trump to become president? Maybe, maybe not. There is absolutely *zero* way to know if this was God's desire. Yet Sarah Sanders (who identifies herself as a Christian) said what she said, as absurd and misleading as it was, and many Trump supporters took it as Gospel and began repeating it as such. Hijacking Christianity.

"I think God calls all of us to fill different roles at different times..." Sarah Sanders https://www.washingtonpost.com/religion/2019/01/30/sarah-sanders-tells-christian-broadcasting-network-god-wanted-trump-be-president/

The second statement, that guns are somehow a God-given right, verges on lunacy. Most certainly the God of Christianity didn't make gun ownership a God-given right. How do I know this? Because *no one had invented guns when the Bible was written.* This is yet another Christianity hijack. Yet Sarah Sanders, a Christian, made these false and misleading statements and numerous Trump supporters heard them from a person of high importance in the Trump White House, and received them as Truth.

Do words and intent matter?

You bet they do.

Let the following story illustrate the importance of speaking truth clearly *and* hearing words accurately.

I Think I Saw a Pig Fly

I was sitting downstairs in my home office. My wife was somewhere upstairs. I was just doing my thing, surfing the web and minding my own business when I heard her voice yelling at me from upstairs, "I think I saw a pig fly!"

I yelled back upstairs, "What?" I waited and then I heard her voice even louder saying, "I think I saw a pig fly!" This made absolutely no sense to me whatsoever. So again I hollered back to her with a somewhat frustratingly perplexed sounding, "WHAT??"

I heard her voice again.

This time at an elevated level echoing through the halls, down the stairs and into my office, "I – THINK – I - SAW – A - PIG – FLY!!!!!!!!" My reaction is somewhat like yours probably is right now – the dots just aren't connecting. And given that we neither own pigs nor do pigs have wings, either my wife has gone completely crazy or something truly miraculous has taken place. Confused, curious and a tad bit irritated, I got up from my computer, walked around the corner, poked my head up the stairwell and said to her one more time, "What . Did . You . Say???"

My wife now sounds angry. But in one instant it all makes perfect sense to me as she says in an exasperated voice, "This House Looks Like a Pig Sty!"

Oh.

I have finally understood. I have heard correctly. The world is as it should be. Pigs do not fly. But our house looks like a pig sty. I get it. Being married is both a cool and confusing game to play sometimes.

But the fun doesn't end there. Nope. Even though I have now understood the *literal* meaning of what she is saying I must quickly decipher *why* she is saying it. I need to understand her full and intended meaning. Is she simply trying to inform me of our messy house? Or is she implying that I am to blame for the mess? OR, does the phrase "this house looks like a pig sty" actually mean "Dean, I want you to clean up your sloppy mess now."

It's tough sometimes to know the true meaning behind what we hear or what we read. Even in the Bible, to fully understand the true meaning of ancient scripture, we need to know both *what* was said and also understand *why* it was said. We need context. In addition, we must have some basic comprehension of the way words were used thousands of years ago to be able to grasp some of the meanings that may have been lost through the Greek and

Hebrew translations.

I think Jesus wants us to be very, *very* careful how we say things and how we interpret things. In reality, the only way we can have a chance at interpreting ancient Biblical writings is through the power of the Holy Spirit living in us. As Jesus said, *"the Counselor, the Holy Spirit, whom the Father will send in my name, will teach you all things and will remind you of everything I have said to you." (John 14:26)*

To those of you reading who are not Christian let me add some clarity about the Holy Spirit stuff. Most mainline Christians believe that the Holy Spirit, God living in us, interprets the teachings of Jesus for us. I know that sounds weird. But stay with me. The idea is that without the Holy Spirit (the Spirit of God) living in our hearts and minds we cannot correctly interpret the Bible. Without the Holy Spirit giving all those ancient writings context and meaning, pointing us toward their intended life-application connections, the Bible is simply an academic study. It is merely words written on pages with nothing but literal and historical analysis to draw from. And since much of the Bible's Old Testament was written in Ancient Hebrew, a language that no longer exists, extracting an accurate interpretation from a literal reading is virtually impossible.

I should also add that the *discernment* of God's voice within the heart and mind of a believer is of the utmost importance. We all have thoughts, bias, personal agenda, along with political and religious agendas that can distort or even fully block what the Holy Spirit is trying to say to us. This is why we need context (and honest self-awareness). If what we are hearing doesn't fall within the parameters of *loving one another* and *the loving and caring for all people* - integral values of Jesus Christ - then it is probably a false voice.

The point here is this: Christian leaders and Christians need to speak very clearly and carefully the Truth. Not some concocted twisting of scripture to suit their own political agenda. (As it would appear Sarah Sanders did in her two aforementioned statements.)

The world is watching us. The world is listening.

Maybe Sarah Sanders actually believes that God was talking

specifically about guns and the United States constitution when He spoke to Moses, the prophets and through Jesus. If so, cool. She is entitled to her own belief system. But if she was just using God and twisting Bible scriptures to sell a political agenda, I would plead with her - stop it!

You are hijacking Christianity and hurting Jesus.

Danger

I've been working day and night lately trying to finish up this book, but certain politicians and Christian Leaders keep saying ridiculous stuff, anti-Jesus stuff, that I feel must be addressed. Some of the statements are quite dangerous like this one that I read last night.

> *"If the Democrats are successful in removing the president from office, I'm afraid it will cause a Civil War-like fracture in this nation from which this country will never heal."*

This was stated by Pastor Robert Jeffress and then tweeted with only a couple of word changes by the President himself.

I'm like, what?

You don't have to be a Christian or a Republican or a Democrat to know how dangerous and goofed up that statement is. First of all, the democrats cannot remove Trump from office. As of this writing they control the House of Representatives so they can impeach him but the Senate would have to vote to convict. The senate is currently controlled by Republicans so, quite obviously, a Democrat and Republican united super majority would need to vote to remove the President from office.

But that's not the most goofed up part.

The goofiest part is the dog whistle context in which Robert

Jeffress and Donald Trump are conveying their message. The obvious intended meaning is: *If the Democrats remove Trump from office there may be Civil War.*

I find it unbelievably distressing that a person who holds the title of "Christian pastor" or "President of the United States" would stoke the fires of fear, plant the seeds of anger and fuel the engines of rage in their followers in such a divisive manner. That they would recklessly suggest the possibility of a "Civil War-like fracture" if congressional discovery uncovers high crimes and misdemeanors enough to warrant impeachment and removal from office. Words matter. Their words and tweets are disgraceful. It's as if they actually want bullets to fly. It's as if they are threatening to signal a call to arms. It's as if... as if neither really knows Jesus at all.

Jesus is about love, peace and unity.

Trump and Jeffress are citing a "Civil War" in their fear mongering. Don't they understand that the Civil War was *Americans* killing *Americans*? Is that what they want?

Truly great leaders always seek to ease tensions and strive for unity.

These guys are seeking to increase tensions and are promoting divisiveness by appealing to human nature's worst tendencies.

This is anti-Jesus.

And it is astonishing.

Fake News

Fake and Bake

Fortunately, the United States of America is a country of free speech.

Unfortunately, the United States is a country of free speech.

(I am, of course, exaggerating here to make a point.)

We are fortunate in the United States to be able to freely speak our minds. We can openly share our hearts, our thoughts, our opinions and our words as long as they are not a targeted threat. We are lucky to be able to practice our religions whatever they may be without fear of being imprisoned or stoned to death.

This freedom of speech is a precious imperative for any country striving to be a democracy. There are still many countries around the world where dictators or authoritarians not only lambast the free press but imprison or put to death those who give opposing views to their doctrine. If these dictators don't want to be seen as murderous they will still most always accuse opposing voices of not having their facts correct.

Unfortunately, there has been a surge of this type of authoritarian expression in the United States recently. The term "Fake News" is getting thrown around like confetti at a parade by some with no evidence to back up their claims.

The constant barrage of this type of behavior has severely undermined and eroded the public's trust in the factual, multi-sourced news reported by journalists doing their best to have no bias in their coverage. This undermining of public trust is indeed the primary intent of those alleging "fake news" without any evidence to back up their claims. Their ploy is regrettably working.

God calls this type of behavior "bearing false witness." Currently, certain conservative Christians and Christian leaders seem to have no trouble supporting those who engage in bearing false witness by deceitfully claiming legitimate news to be fake. This is another hijacking of Christianity.

Jesus Christ doesn't like lies. They're not on his playlist. He is not too fond of people bearing false witness against one another nor does He rejoice when people spin facts, propagate falsehoods, or fabricate narratives with the intent of misleading others. When you see this happening you can be sure that Jesus is being wounded. Engaging in such rhetorical promiscuity is most certainly not of Christ, and Christian leaders supporting politicians who participate in such behavior need to call them out.

But instead of calling out the lies, bearing false witness and the belittling of others, I've heard Christian leaders simply throw around softball phrases like, "I wouldn't say it that way," or "I don't like some of his tweets," or "I wish he wouldn't tweet so much." Ladies and gentleman, those are weak responses from supposedly strong Christian leaders. Every time the world witnesses such pathetic leadership you can almost hear a collective refrain singing, "The Christian ship is sinking."

Divided States

In the age of Trump, as the people of the United States have become more and more divided and more tribal in their political views, the temptation to tell lies or to spin facts has been growing. With the advent of social media, any person with access to the Internet can put forth whatever nutty views they want. Indeed, in this era of immediate access, the spread of misinformation, falsehoods, and tribal-cultivating spins has been rampant. Unfortunately, this has had the adverse effect of dividing people instead of uniting them.

This is not good. At least according to Jesus. I don't think He was joking around when He said, *"If a house is divided against itself, that house cannot stand." (Mark 3:25)*

Again, let me be absolutely clear about a couple of things having to do with Jesus Christ. First of all, Jesus is not a fan of people telling lies, twisting facts or propagating falsehoods. In addition, it is most certainly anti-Jesus to attempt to breed divisiveness amongst people. Jesus wants unity. He wants to bring people together.

Free speech in the United States is a precious and necessary right. Free speech is also necessary in order to maintain a true democracy. It does, however, open up a can of worms and gives a megaphone to anyone with twisted thoughts or ill-intent.

In this day and age of easily accessible social media and twenty-four hour cable "news" channels, there is no easy solution to the problem of the viral spread of falsehoods and lies. I can only hope that our better nature will someday win out.

We currently have a president in the White House, Donald Trump, who proclaims his Christianity. We also currently have a president in the White House, Donald Trump, who according to the Washington Post has made false or misleading claims over 16,000 times in three years. At the same he has used the phrase "fake news" seemingly anytime he doesn't like what a particular multi-sourced, factual news story says.

If one analyzes Donald Trump's use of the phrase *fake news* one quickly discovers he utilizes it most often as a weapon against stories that put him in a disparaging light. This is unfortunate for the United States of America. And as conservative Evangelical leaders continue to brush off this behavior as inconsequential they are devaluing the words and teachings of Jesus Christ.

There are many who would like me to say that you *can't* support Donald Trump if you are a Christian. And many who would like me to say that you *must* support Donald Trump if you are a Christian. But neither of those assertions would be correct. You *can't* or you *must* is not what this is about. If you are a Christian or a Christian leader who supports *any politician* who is a serial offender in making false statements, bearing false witness, and belittling others, you simply must call out this type of behavior as being what it is: unacceptable. If you do not, Christianity gets wounded. And worst of all, Jesus Christ gets wounded.

To remain silent in the face of these serial sins while fully supporting the sinner is to be complicit. Jesus wasn't silent. In fact, His actions and His words got him killed. When stuff is blatantly wrong it needs to be stated as such.

Do we all have bad behavior or improper thoughts at times? Of course we do. That is part of being bound by and to our own flawed humanity. I cannot recount all of the things I have thought or done in my life that would be considered sinful. I would need to write an entire library of books to document them all. What we are talking about here, however, is *serial* bad behavior. Continual sacrilege. Consistent wrongdoing with no repentance whatsoever.

I have witnessed many Christian leaders attempt to sweep these types of divisive actions, misleading statements and claims of *fake news* under the rug or justify them by saying we need to have Donald Trump leading our country for the "greater good." That is poppycock. You cannot be achieving a greater good by leading people in a manipulative way. Jesus calls His disciples to love, to be caring, to have integrity, virtue and dignity.

It is my strong belief that some of those same Christians who are sweeping this profane behavior under the rug need to have a "come to Jesus" moment of their own. Then maybe they'll understand the need to call out the one they support and hold him up to a higher moral standard. Indeed, *they are the ones* who may be able to hold him accountable. Maybe *they* can encourage him to have a turning of the heart and mind. A repentance, if you will.

Granted, there are numerous Christian leaders who are calling Donald Trump to a higher moral standard. They are the Christian leaders who are *not* hijacking their religion and are doing their best to be true to their Lord and Savior, Jesus Christ. To them I say, *well done good and faithful servants.*

Media

It has been quite disheartening to watch some of the "news" media outlets sacrificing their integrity for the sake of an audience (i.e., money). I guess this is their Golden Calf. Please don't think that I am naïve about media organizations. I know that money is a primary driving factor and even the best journalists have at least some bias. We all do. But now more than ever I truly appreciate the media outlets and personnel who strive to be as fact based and unbiased as possible.

What I would say to those media organizations and the people in them who are conspiring to spin falsehoods, creating false narratives, misleading people, or outright lying for the sake of profit or political gain is this: There is no justifying this type of behavior as somehow serving any greater good. Misleading people never serves a greater good no matter what justification one uses.

If there are media personnel engaged in this type of activity who also wave the Christian flag as part of their identity, they are

Dean Krippaehne

unequivocally hijacking Christianity. Non-believers who look at them, who see them, who witness their misleading activity day in and day out, get the idea that Christians will lie, cheat, mislead, misinform and do most anything to advance their own political agenda or media career. This is a total hijack and it is pounding another nail into the hand (or wrist) of Jesus Christ on the cross.

I am not saying that Donald Trump or any of the media who engage in lies, falsehoods, or misleading information are not Christian. Christians just like everyone else fall short sometimes. What I am saying is that their *behavior* in these ways is not of Jesus Christ. And they need to change their behavior.

I hope and pray every day that Donald Trump and the conservative Evangelical leaders who unabashedly support him without calling out his falsehoods, as well as some in the media who are misleading the public, will at some point, somehow and in some way have their hearts transformed by Christ.

Lies, falsehoods, misinformation, fake news and propaganda only serve to imprison us to the sins that they are.

Being a media outlet of integrity (or a President of integrity) is really simple if you want to break it down to its essence. First of all, stop bearing false witness and calling truthful news fake news. Secondly, plain and simple: *tell the truth*. It really is that straightforward.

Cattle in Seattle

It was a summer job between my freshman and sophomore years of college. Being a suburbia-skater-boy type kid I had never done anything even remotely like it. This particular summer I would be taking care of one-hundred head of cattle on a small farm just outside of Seattle, Washington.

I loved it. I loved getting up at 4:30 each fresh, summer morning. I

76

loved making my way to the farm's grain shed by five. I loved driving down the long dirt road toward the main barn and past the old wooden fence that stretched the entire length of a lazy, open grazing field. I was amazed that after just a couple of short weeks of coming to the farm each day, the cattle, upon seeing and hearing my old and embarrassingly noisy Chevy Vega, would start heading toward the barn anticipating the breakfast I was about to provide.

I remember how they would look up at me with their big cow eyes as I would fill their trough with hay and grain. I could almost see their grateful smiles and hear them say "thank you good buddy." They really did seem to like me. Their ears twitching in affectionate response as I would talk to them. They were like giant-size puppy dogs wagging their tails in unconditional love for their favorite human. Each one clamoring and positioning himself for my very best attention.

One thing was for sure, in just a very short time they grew to trust me completely. They trusted me to care for them, to feed them, to give them water when they were thirsty, and to provide a huge open field where they could graze and roam freely doing pretty much as they pleased.

That summer I was their whole world and they knew I wouldn't let them down. By the end of the season they would have followed me almost anywhere in Cattleville.

Little did they know, however, what my real intentions were. That the good life they were living, the fat and happy times, were not quite what they seemed. They had no idea that a much different fate was soon awaiting them.

I loved taking care of those one-hundred cattle. They ate up everything I could possibly feed them. Had they known their eventual fate, the inevitable consequence of their good times, they would have undoubtedly headed for the hills just as fast as their little legs could carry them.

My seemingly nice and loving ways were in reality nothing more than lies they had fallen for. Yes, they soon were to become... well... dead meat.

Who to Trust

As God's children living in a flawed world we've got to be able to discern who to trust and who to be wary of. There will always be a lot of people *feeding* us a lot of different things. We must be able to recognize that what may *seem* good for us may actually bring us destruction in the end. And we must be able to act upon that knowledge.

Sometimes it is easy to tell the difference between the good stuff and the bad stuff. Sometimes, however, the bad stuff has been so cleverly disguised it is hard to distinguish it from the good. It's like we need a code-breaker or a translator or an anti-virus program to differentiate truth from fiction. We need someone who can be our eyes and ears when we cannot perceive evil. Someone who will warn us when harm is near.

Here is the key. If what you are hearing, watching or reading has at its core love and caring for all people, inclusiveness and kindness, it is probably trustworthy. The good stuff. If it does not mislead, belittle, or lie, it is also most likely trustworthy. If it does not bear false witness, brag or boast, or show signs of envy or jealousy, it is indeed honorable. Why? Because these are all things of God.

However, if what you are witnessing has at its core: fear, hate, conspiracy, claims without credible evidence, bragging, boastfulness, false statements, rumors, innuendo, divisive language, rudeness and belittlement... run far and fast away. It is not trustworthy nor is it of God. It is of the other dude.

Also, if we perform our due diligence, if we have patience and uncover facts, we will be better armed to fight the onslaught of misinformation being fed to us by unsavory types.

Lastly, if we find our spiritual leaders wrapping themselves in Godly words while at the same time being complicit in hiding pertinent facts or supporting those pushing falsehoods and misinformation, we need to call them out and call *them* up to God.

Jesus said, "Beware *of false prophets, who come to you in sheep's clothing but inwardly are ravenous wolves." - (Matthew 7:15)*

We must keep our eyes open.

Observations on Fake News

Like it or not, we currently find ourselves living in a day and age where the kind of gossipy trash once reserved for grocery store checkout line titillation (i.e. The National Enquirer-type sensationalism) now shows up every hour (every minute) in our social media news feed as well as on cable news opinion shows. Unfortunately, many people have succumbed to the temptation of accepting much of this National Enquirerism as fact based, legitimate news. Especially when it supports their personal bias.

Consequently, it has never been more important to seek out facts first and to educate ourselves on a variety of issues for the purpose of guarding against consuming misinformation. If we are to cultivate a strong, healthy and mature culture, nurturing this type of discipline is paramount. Never before has due diligence in researching a broad scope of reporting from a wide breadth of reliable sources been more important. For any country to retain a free society built upon a foundation of integrity and rectitude, a vigilant citizenry is an absolute imperative.

We have entered a brand new paradigm in the cultural wars. Those now lying on the battlefield do not have bodily wounds but rather wounds of the mind and its ability to reason. They have been rendered dazed and confused, having been hit again and again by unscrupulous word twisters with nefarious intent.

It is incumbent upon those of us who value civility and meaningful discourse to encourage those swayed by modern hyperbole to triple-check fact sources. Are the accounts of what you are reading or watching firsthand? Are the sources reliable? Are stories objectively reported and vetted to the standards of traditional news? Are there other reliable news organizations corroborating the information? What are the reporting organizations gaining from their headlines (viewership, money, power, influence)? Does that come into play or influence the framing of their story? And finally: Who is financing any particular media entity and what is *their* bias?

Nothing less than the Truth is at stake as we move forward.

Jesus doesn't like lies.

Fox, Fear, Falsehoods and Faith

As we move into this next section I would like to recall once again the words of Jesus:

"If anyone causes one of these little ones - those who believe in me - to stumble, it would be better for them to have a large millstone hung around their neck and to be drowned in the depths of the sea." (Matthew 18: 6)

Sasquatch

As a teenager living in Washington State I had heard the myths. I was well aware of the rumors and stories about the big hairy monster living in our hills. You know, Bigfoot. It seems silly now but at the time my friends and I were all gullible, looking for adventure and curious about these Sasquatch stories. We even convinced ourselves that they were probably true. We would often sit around fantasizing that maybe *we* would be the ones to finally capture a picture of a real, living Sasquatch. Without dying in the process.

Such is the way of a young and naive teenager's mind sometimes.

I remember one night when four or five of us packed ourselves into a car and drove deep into the Western Washington woods. We had decided to go Sasquatch hunting. We didn't have any weapons or anything like that. We weren't going to try to shoot one. We'd just convinced ourselves that on this dark, damp and foggy night a Sasquatch most surely would appear in the woods and we would finally be able to snap a picture of it.

Our car seemed to almost drive itself down the deserted roads as if being pulled by some unseen force of nature. In and around twists and turns we went, creeping through the thick fog, barely staying on the pavement until we came upon a slight clearing in the woods. It was there that we parked our car, got out and began walking and stalking the supposed Sasquatch through the forest.

I don't know if you've ever been on an adventure in the middle-of-nowhere on a deep, dark night but I can tell you that it feels pretty creepy to the imaginative mind. Long story short, nothing really happened that night other than a bunch of young teenagers scaring themselves half to death. Every snap of a twig, every unfamiliar creak, every strange chirp or squeal from some pine marmot or raccoon had us shaking in our sneakers thinking a Sasquatch was upon us. But it was all in our imaginations. When you are in the dark, the unseen can take on a life of its own.

We would repeat these adventures every now and then and I'm pretty sure we were not alone. Most likely teenagers in every part of the world, especially where there have been reports of Sasquatch sightings, have gone out in the middle of the night to entertain themselves by being scared silly. The power of myth, rumors and unsubstantiated legends can do that. Being in the dark with a wild imagination can be both exciting and terrifying.

This is how I have come to feel about some of the opinion hosts on one of the cable "news" networks. Not that they are monsters or at all terrifying but that they deal largely in myth, rumor and conspiracy theory as a means to excite and terrify their audience.

Yes, there are commentators on every network who have a bit of bias and spin but today I'm going to pick on a network called Fox News because in my opinion no cable network currently employs a few commentator-hosts with a more egregious spin on truth than does the Fox News Channel. (I guess I just lost any possibility of their endorsement. Oh darn.)

I won't name the particular hosts who are continually stimulating their viewers with the most abhorrent twisting of facts, but as I have watched and listened to some of them and fact-checked their assertions, I have come to the conclusion that many are operating in much the same way my friends and I did as young teenagers when we were letting our imaginations run wild out in the woods.

It's as if every evening they climb into their hour-long TV-cars and take their audience down a dark and foggy path in the middle of the night, entertaining, frightening and exciting them with myth, rumor, innuendo and conspiracy nonsense about political Sasquatches. They convince themselves and their audience that there are monsters out there that are very real, nearby, and intend to do everyone harm.

It's a sad state of affairs when grown adults buy into myth and insinuation the same way we might have done as young teenagers. I understand why they do it. Propagating conspiracy theories to reinforce political bias is a giant cash cow (a Golden Calf, if you will) for both the network and its hosts. They know that if they spin a political Sasquatch yarn as if it were factual that many of their viewers through excitement, fear or anger will be entertained enough to believe these tales as true. They know, too, that as their viewers tune in night after night to feed their addiction, advertisers will pay enormous sums of money to sell their products to those same gullible and misled viewers.

It is even more regretful that some in the religious right have fallen under the spell of this kind of adolescent, unprincipled buffoonery. They have bought into it hook, line and sinker and are now leading their flocks astray. That they are doing it all in the name of Jesus is disheartening.

Let me assure you that Jesus Christ is not about fear or being in the dark and the fog, nor is He about being entertained and excited by Sasquatch myths or unsubstantiated conspiracy theories. *Jesus only deals in love, which is the opposite of fear, and in truth, which is the opposite of lies.* Jesus Christ is not about spinning a yarn for the sake of audience and profit. Nor is He about telling half-truths to garner prestige and political power.

If one wants to tell their tales, spin their yarns and engage in myth and rumor spreading, so be it. If a network wants to deal in propaganda, conspiracy theories and fear as their viewership addiction model for the purpose of making a profit, they are legally allowed to do so. I don't agree with this type of behavior, but it is their prerogative in a free society to engage in such. But to those networks and opinion hosts who cannot refrain from this type of mind manipulation and sociological malfeasance, I ask you one simple thing: Leave Jesus out of it. Stop hijacking Christianity for the sake of a buck.

Of course, there will always be some who would say Sasquatches are real. To them my response is... Cool. Give me proof.

Are You Freaking Kidding Me?

Here is another statement from Robert Jeffress:

> *"I am not saying that President Obama is the Antichrist. ... But what I am saying is this: the course he is choosing to lead our nation is paving the way for the future reign of the Antichrist."*

There is just so much wrong about this statement. It implies that President Obama was paving the way for the Antichrist. Are you freaking kidding me? The Bible was pretty clear about "bearing false witness" being a no-no. So, although I would never call Robert Jeffress the Antichrist, I will firmly state that what he is insinuating here and the way he is misleading people is anti-Jesus.

Here's the deal...

Robert Jeffress can disagree with President Obama if he wants to. He can paint him in a disparaging light if he wishes. That's just politics. He can pontificate his political spins on Fox News if he so desires. But I'll guarantee that he cannot provide *one shred of hard evidence* backing up his claim of Obama's course (or anyone else's course) paving the way for the Antichrist.

This type of statement from Robert Jeffress is false, misleading, inflammatory and dangerous. The way it plays upon the fears some people have of an Antichrist emerging is nothing but a flimflam con. It is also not of Jesus Christ by any stretch of the imagination, therefore it is another hijack.

If I was Robert Jeffress's mother I might make him was his mouth out with soap for that one. And then have him study both the definition of the word "deceiver" and what the Bible has to say about those who deceive others. Heck, if I was his Sunday school teacher I would most likely make him write "I promise to stop deceiving others" seventy-times-seven consecutive times on the chalkboard.

To Whom It May Concern...

We can do better than this. We must be better than this. As Christian leaders there is no need to stoke the fires of the mentally troubled with deceitful statements. There is also no need to feed the fears of the spiritually frail with talk of an Antichrist. This kind of behavior is beneath us. All of us. It is beneath our congregations, our country and most certainly our God. We can do better. We must be better.

Watermelon

When I was growing up my mom used to fix and serve watermelon in a very special way. She would always serve fresh watermelon *cubed* with all of the seeds taken out. This was the only way, growing up, that I ever ate watermelon. For all I knew watermelon actually grew in little, pinkish-red cubes, without seeds. As far as I was concerned you could just pop those tasty, cubed bites into your mouth right off the vine. I'm sure I must have seen watermelon at the grocery store or on TV but I never really thought about it.

Consequently, when I grew up and got married, I was startled the first time my wife cut up and served watermelon one hot summer day. I was aghast at how goofy looked. I mean, she served it in these half-moon shapes, about an inch thick, with a weird, green outer layer attached. Each piece had a bunch of black seeds in the reddish-pink part. It kind of looked like watermelon but the seeds really threw me. When I asked my wife how I was supposed to get the seeds out, the look on her face told me that our young marriage might be in jeopardy should I ever ask that question again.

I quickly figured out the seed thing on my own.

Then kept my mouth shut.

We're still married.

We all have limited life experience. It's crazy how we sometimes think that our own particular way of viewing things is the *only* way to view them. Sadly, we sometimes criticize or judge others who simply see things a bit differently than we do, telling them they are wrong, when they are simply looking at stuff through the prism of *their* own personal life experience.

So many battles are fought because of this. So many people are wounded. So many families, friends, communities, even countries are divided because we refuse to entertain the possibility that there may be another way, a different perspective, a unique pair of shoes we have yet to walk in.

Sure, there are things in life that are absolutes - right or wrong, black or white. But there are also innumerable things in life that are not black or white. Events that can be viewed, experienced and thought of in a variety of different ways.

Let us always seek to understand one another's diverse points of view. This is what healthy people do. But let us also understand that there are times when things are black or white, right or wrong. Times when a well-researched and evidenced fact is indeed a fact, and when the truth is the truth and when a lie is a lie.

Here are just a few (of the thousands) of provably false statements made by Donald Trump. The only reason I cannot call these lies is that I cannot prove Donald Trump's *intent* when he made these and so many other factually false statements.

* "Yesterday we had the strongest dollar in the history of our country."
Nope, not even close. False statement!

* U.S. farmers are receiving $16 billion "out of the tariffs that we've gotten from China."
Nope. China is not paying U.S. farmers $16B through tariffs. False statement!

* "Mexico, they took 30% of our automobile business."

Nope. False statement!

* "Our Economy is the best it has ever been. Best Employment & Stock Market Numbers EVER." Nope. False statement! (Debunked by numerous economists)

* Trump said that when his supporters chanted "send her back" about Ilhan Omar, he stopped it.
Nope. Video shows otherwise. False statement!

* (per Twitter blocking his followers) "I know that we've been blocked. People come up to me and they say, 'Sir, I can't get you - I can't follow you. They make it impossible."
Nope. A ten second Google search proves this statement false.

* The United Kingdom is "our largest (trading) partner."
Nope. It ranks fifth. False statement!

(Note: Citations for each of these above falsehoods can be found in the "notes" section at the end of this book - they can also be easily googled)

Why do I point these relatively mild falsehoods (possibly lies) out? Because there are still Christians who insist that Donald Trump has never made a false claim or lied while in office.

It should be noted that a few of the personalities on Fox News have either backed up or spun in misleading ways some of these and many other false claims made by President Trump.

I don't know about you, but I tend to become more than a little irritated when politicians and media personalities start throwing around falsehoods on a regular basis. I become especially upset when faith leaders *fan the flames of fear* with misleading arguments. I go bat-crap crazy when faith leaders start making idols out of political policy - as if their particular political slant is the true church of Christianity. Here's another statement made by

Christian Evangelical Pastor Robert Jeffress as reported in The Washington Post:

"When Trump used the word "sh*thole" to describe African and other nations earlier this year? No big deal."

No big deal?

That is a racist statement.
Coming from the president of the United States.

A little context. Michael Cohen, Donald Trump's longtime lawyer testified before congress and under oath that Donald Trump once asked him if he *"could name a country run by a black person that wasn't a 'shithole'."*

Would Jesus Christ think it is OK to describe countries as "shithole" countries?

Robert Jeffress is a Christian Pastor.

Another hijack.

Lying

Here's the deal about lying: Anyone can do it if they want to. It's everyone's prerogative. You can lie about little things. You can lie about great big life altering things. You can tell half-truths and mislead people and say that you're not lying. But if you do so knowingly, that is the definition of lying.

You are even free to convince yourself that you're not lying because of some greater purpose. That's still lying. You can justify almost any lie by saying "something more important" is at stake, therefore you need to mislead people so that this important thing can get accomplished. Yup, this too is lying. Often that's not just lying to other people, that is lying to yourself.

You can double down on a lie, but the lie you told is still a lie. You can even triple-down on the lie you told. But all that does is turn your lie into a lie that you told three times.

Lying is not good no matter when or how it's done. In fact, in the Bible Jesus refers to Satan (the devil) as *"the father of lies." (John 8:44)* I wouldn't want to be put in the same camp as Satan, the father of lies. I'd rather be in the other camp. The camp of the Good Shepherd. The camp of Truth. The camp of Jesus.

It's a tricky thing sometimes to accuse others of lying without being hypocritical. If we're honest with ourselves, we know that from time to time we all tell little white lies. Our little white lies might not seem significant in the big picture of life but they still have a way of eating away at our integrity and damaging our character.

A serial liar is another thing altogether. At least here in this world. It destroys trust, erodes confidence, leads others astray and confuses people in such a way that there is no longer any common ground of facts and truth upon which we can communicate and reason from. It divides and tears apart and deceives and destroys all that is good. Yeah, serial lying is a *really* big deal and a *really* bad thing.

Lying, misleading people and twisting facts are behaviors we need to avoid if we want to be people of integrity. If we want to have a society of integrity and be people of healthy moral character, if we desire to let truth be the foundation upon which we stand, lying can't be a part of our vernacular. From a Christian perspective it should be noted that every time we engage in lying or support someone else's lying habit we harm our Lord, Jesus Christ

The call Jesus places upon His disciples is that of Truth.

Sometimes Christ followers need to be the voice of Jesus throwing His spear of Truth into the heart of a lie. It is not casting stones to call out wrong doing. It is not being overly judgmental to let a liar know that what they are engaging in is anti-Jesus. It is not wrong to protect those being harmed by lies by challenging the liar's false assertions. We simply *must* call out someone who engages in serial lying. For the sake of all and for the sake of the liar we must give them the opportunity to change, to turn away from their deceptiveness.

It is one thing to lie, to be called out, to make a turn and then try to not lie again. It is quite another thing to lie, to be called out, and then to double down on that lie with yet another lie. In that case there has been no repentance, no turning away from the deceptive action, and no turning towards the Truth.

We are living in such a time now. I've called this time in history the Age of Trump. I could probably also refer to it as the age of doubling down on lies. As I've stated before, the Washington Post has a running count of misleading statements and falsehoods made by Donald Trump during his candidacy and as President of the United States. As of this writing there are over 16,000 such falsehoods and misleading statements - all made by the very same person - Donald Trump.

There are also numerous other falsehoods, misleading statements, or what I would call lies by those who work for and support the current President of the United States. Literally hundreds of such misleading statements and falsehoods. It's crazy. One of Donald Trump's surrogates, Corey Lewandowski, testified before congress in September of 2019 that, "I have no obligation to be honest with the media." Wow! His obvious motive was to protect himself and the one (Trump) making the lies in the first place. So, Donald Trump's dishonesty begets more dishonesty. Trump's lies beget more lies. Trump's misleading statements beget more misleading statements. It is a vicious circle and a destructive cycle that Satan, the father of lies, relishes and revels in.

It is simply astonishing to me that some of Trump's Christian supporters are not calling out this behavior. When they remain silent, Satan chuckles. To them I say - call him out! Let me say it again, *call out these lies*. Call him *up to a higher standard*. Don't brush aside or sweep falsehoods under the rug. Don't say they don't matter. They do. They are eroding his heart, they are misleading and eroding the hearts of his supporters causing them to lie for him and double down for him. They are eroding the moral fiber, dignity and integrity of our country. And what distresses me most of all is the sad reality that they are hijacking the Word of Jesus Christ.

Jesus is a voice for the voiceless, not a megaphone for the rich and powerful.

61% of white evangelicals found Donald Trump "Morally Upstanding"

*Pew Research Center study released March 10th, 2020

* NPR reports Pew Study https://www.npr.org/2020/03/12/815097747/survey-most-evangelicals-see-trump-as-honest-and-morally-upstanding
* Full Pew Research Center Study
https://www.pewforum.org/2020/03/12/white-evangelicals-see-trump-as-fighting-for-their-beliefs-though-many-have-mixed-feelings-about-his-personal-conduct/?utm_source=adaptivemailer&utm_medium=email&utm_campaign=20-03-12%20religion%20and%202020%20election&org=982&lvl=100&ite=5702&lea=1272618&ctr=0&par=1&trk=
* 61 percent find Trump "Morally Upstanding"
https://www.pewforum.org/2020/03/12/white-evangelicals-see-trump-as-fighting-for-their-beliefs-though-many-have-mixed-feelings-about-his-personal-conduct/pf_03-12-20_religion-politics-00-9/

Kids in Cages

"...and whoever gives even a cup of cold water to one of these little ones in the name of a disciple – truly I tell you, none of these will lose their reward..." (Matthew 10:42)

Imagine hundreds, no, *thousands* of children coming across the southern border of the United States. Imagine they are being brought by their parents who are fleeing violence, trying to escape poverty and just looking for a safe place to live. Imagine those children being separated from their parents and not being told why this was happening. Now imagine those same children, already exhausted from having walked hundreds and hundreds of miles, not being told when or if they will ever get to see their parents again.

It's a horror story.

It's a story of child abuse.

Imagine if you will some of these very same children being kept in what, for all practical purposes, can only be described as *cages*. Imagine these children not having access to any decent, healthy food or medical help or psychological counseling. Imagine the parents of these children, now in an unknown location, wondering what has happened to their little ones, where they are, if they are safe or if they will ever even see them again. Picture in your mind these children who are not being given proper medical care, still in their caged quarters, and now contracting diseases from one another. Some are becoming extremely sick. Imagine some of them dying.

Now imagine Jesus.

Imagine Jesus turning his back on these children and doing nothing. Imagine Jesus supporting the ones who are responsible for the traumatization of these children without speaking out. Imagine Jesus turning a blind eye to this inhumane treatment. Imagine Jesus justifying this cruel behavior that is being inflicted upon these innocent children.

I know, right?

Jesus would never, ever, *ever* turn his back on these children. Jesus Christ would *not* be ok with this type of inhumane treatment of anyone, let alone children.

And yet it is happening.

There are even some Evangelical leaders who have effectively turned their back on these children. There are some Christians and Christian leaders who are turning a blind eye or somehow justifying this insidious behavior. There are some conservative Evangelicals who are leading their flocks in such a way that they are not only supporting and praising the ones responsible for traumatizing these children, but are claiming that the leader of this travesty has been appointed by God to make this country great.

Are you kidding me?

This is not greatness. It is evil.

And indeed this is what is happening in the United States of America.

WTF

I honestly never thought I would ever again see or hear about this particular flavor of institutionalized evil in my country. Seeing kids in cages. Yet here we are. I'm extraordinarily disheartened by the many who support it or support the ones implementing it. The type of dehumanization rhetoric and actions we are witnessing at the direction of the current administration has played itself out many times in history. We've seen this movie before. We've read the book. We know where it leads and how it ends if left unchecked.

And yet it is happening.

And there are many who wear the name "Christian" who are supporting these efforts.

We've also seen that movie before.

Granted, it's a very difficult challenge dealing with immigration, asylum seekers and refugees, but finding a humane way to treat people shouldn't be a challenge. I know that it takes money to care for those in need but the United States has the money to do so. And once you've allocated the money it should be pretty straight forward how to treat people. Treat them the way you would want to be treated.

That is what Jesus would do.

Dean Krippaehne

Freedom in the Spiritual

Because there are some reading this book who do not know Jesus, I want to offer the following on their behalf.

God is in the liberation business. God is in the freedom business. God wants us to be liberated from sin. To be free from being enslaved to sin. Mainline Christian theology proposes that all of humanity is sinful and broken. We are imprisoned by our heredity of sin. We cannot free ourselves. But God has given us the key that unlocks the chains and pries open the bars that bind us. In Christianity, the life, death and resurrection of Jesus is that key. And through Jesus Christ we have been set free.

A bit more on God's intention for us.

God is not in the business of locking us up or putting us in cages. God is not in the business of building a wall around us to keep us held as prisoners.

God wants us to be free, unchained and unbound by sin. This is the essence of God's desire for humankind. And it is fundamental in the Christian faith. So this idea that any of us should be put in cages here on earth or in the spiritual realm - or that we can put others in cages - is anti-God. Anti-Jesus.

Religion at its very best is a tool we can use to get to know God more intimately. Religion at its very worst is yet another cage, another box to be trapped in or another sledge hammer with which to bash people who don't agree with a particular interpretation of God.

One needs to be very careful when speaking in absolutes about Christianity. Making a list of dos and don'ts and saying a person cannot get into heaven unless they follow this list is missing the point. What the Bible reveals doesn't hold a candle to the importance of *Who* the Bible reveals, namely Jesus. All too often preachers who list dos and don'ts as a prerequisite for entering the Kingdom of Heaven are just boxing in their congregants. Putting them in spiritual cages. They are constructing religious prison bars and locking their flocks in chains with the intent of controlling them and making them conform to a certain belief. This is incompatible with the teachings of Jesus. Jesus didn't demand that we follow Him. It was and is an *invitation*. Those who instruct in a "conform or else" manner are usually the ones who have a vested interest in maintaining power by keeping things just as they are.

God is way bigger than their twisted, controlling ideas. God is way bigger than cages. God simply IS. "I AM," God said. And the great "I Am" longs for us to be free and non-caged, non-boxed and non-walled off from His/Her liberation. Jesus wants to build a bridge between us and the *Great I Am* that God is. In fact, He wants even more than that. Jesus wants us to be one. Jesus said, *"That all of them may be one, Father, just as You are in Me and I Am in You."* *(John 17:21)*

We must keep a watchful eye out for those who would attempt to box us up with their insular Biblical interpretations or lock us in cages with their list of demands. Beware those who idolize doctrine and denigrate opposing views. All too often they are missing the great invitation God extends to all of us to come and see, to come and follow, to come and believe so that we may be liberated from the shackles of despair and the ties that bind.

My great hope is that all the Christian powers that be can come into the knowledge and understanding that God longs for His preachers, teachers and children everywhere to be liberated and to come together in love as one. This is my prayer. This is my hope.

This is my dream.

Where is the Compassion?

Where is the compassion from the politicians - who claim to be Christians - for the little children being separated from their parents? Where is the compassion from Fox News opinion hosts - who claim to be Christians - for the kids who are being put in cages? Where is the compassion from some Trump supporting preachers for the people of Puerto Rico when they are decimated by a category 5 hurricane? Where is the compassion for people fleeing their corrupted countries looking for asylum in the United States? Where is the compassion for those who don't look like you, or have the same sexuality you, or have or a different religion than you have?

Where is the compassion?

Where is the compassion for the *other*? Where is the compassion for a gold star family? Where is the simple, common respect, human kindness, and politeness when responding to someone with a differing opinion?

Why are certain Evangelical leaders silent on these issues? Why do they not call out the lack of compassion in the political leaders they publicly support? Why are some condoning this lack of compassionate behavior in their elected officials?

Are certain types of people expendable?

Is Jesus not compassionate? Does Jesus not care about children being separated from their parents? Does Jesus not have compassion for the refugee? Does Jesus not love and welcome those who don't look like, sound like, talk like, or act like you?

Of course Jesus has compassion for ALL people.

Jesus IS compassion.

So why is it that certain Evangelical leaders neglect to call out this administration's lack of compassion for *others*?

Yes, in this case too Christianity has been hijacked by those designating their compassion only for a select few people or a select few causes.

When Church Leaders Flee Jesus

Does it surprise me when Christian leaders walk away from the teachings of Jesus to promote their own agenda? No, not really. Does it surprise me when they walk away from Jesus while claiming they are, in fact, following Him? Nope. After all, the Christian Bible has stories of many walking away or turning their back on Jesus. Especially the religious elites.

Heck, it was the religious elites who had Jesus killed.

The Bible has a story about Jesus in the Garden of Gethsemane. Jesus asks his disciples to stay awake with Him. *They fall asleep.* And then after Jesus was arrested, one of His disciples *denied even knowing Him.* Some of the very people who had the closest relationships with Jesus Christ, in one way or another, "left" Him. So does it surprise me when Christian leaders walk away from Jesus? No. As it was two thousand years ago, so it is today. But it does disappoint me and grieve my heart. Especially when they also lead others away from Jesus.

My great prayer for these "walk away" church leaders is that just as Jesus disciples found their way back to Him, so too will these leaders have a revelation of heart and mind, an authentic "come to Jesus moment," and find their way back.

Yet there is Hope

To those who choose love over hate, take heart. To those who choose inclusiveness over excluding others, take heart. To those who welcome, serve and care for all people regardless of where they came from, what they look like, or what their beliefs are, take heart. You are not alone. Jesus is walking with you.

To those who have sensed that there is something misguided about being a *PowerPoint Christian* or a *Checklist Christian* and have been enlightened to the reality that no one can earn their way into eternal life, take heart. Indeed, salvation is a pure and gracious gift from God. Take heart, for the Kingdom is near.

And to my fellow believers in and followers of Jesus Christ, take heart. This world with all of its wrongs, with all of its hate, with all of its twisted teachings, is also teeming with glorious beauty, transformative miracles and many who radiate God's peace, love, service and joy.

Know that this life is not the end of the story but truly just the beginning. For while the human realm is finite, the Spiritual realm is infinite. To my brothers and sisters walking in the Light, I look forward to meeting you and sharing with you in God's peace and joy one great day. If not in this world, surely in the next.

Christ is with you and with me always.

The Golden Calf

When the people saw that Moses was so long in coming down from the mountain, they gathered around Aaron and said, "Come, make us gods who will go before us. As for this fellow Moses who brought us up out of Egypt, we don't know what has happened to him. "Aaron answered them, "Take off the gold earrings that your wives, your sons and your daughters are wearing, and bring them to me." So all the people took off their earrings and brought them to Aaron. He took what they handed him and made it into an idol cast in the shape of a calf, fashioning it with a tool. Then they said, "These are your gods, Israel, who brought you up out of Egypt."

Then the LORD said to Moses, "Go down, because your people, whom you brought up out of Egypt, have become corrupt." (Exodus 32: 1-4, 7)

The Golden Calf

We all have our own Golden Calf (or Golden Calves), don't we? Those things we put before Jesus, before God. Even non-Christians have their own Golden Calves - the things they put before the loving and caring for others. If we are honest with ourselves, if we look deeply into the mirror of our hearts and minds, we will discover that much of our life has been put *ahead* of our relationship with God. Ahead of our care and concern for others. This is a part of being human. We all fall short of the great hope that Jesus had for us to seek *first* the Kingdom. Not *second* the Kingdom, or third the Kingdom, or twenty-seventh the Kingdom, but to *seek first the Kingdom (Matthew 6:33)* and then put everything else second.

I know this is one of the great struggles of my life. There are always bills to pay, appointments to keep and projects to work on. We must remember that Jesus didn't say it would be sin that would choke Him out of our lives, He said it would be the *cares of this world (Mark 4:19)*. And indeed, the "cares of the world" can and do snuff Him out of our daily consciousness. All too often.

Even in the healthiest person's life, it's the working of jobs, going to school, worrying about our cat or dog, our car repair, or our favorite sports team that will quite often take first place in our day to day thoughts. It's not so much that we are trying to turn our backs on Jesus, it's just that common sense tells us life's daily struggles and joys are of more immediate concern.

We feel totally justified in taking care of business first. It is after all, the *common sense* thing to do. But we must remember that common sense is not Spiritual sense. What Jesus taught here was *Spiritual sense.* Indeed, we must often put *taking care of business* first in our outer life (even Jesus did that), it is our *inner life* where we must always keep Jesus first.

These teachings of Jesus were never meant for His selfish desire to be worshiped but for *our own benefit.* If we seek first the Kingdom, letting everything else be secondary in our inner life as Jesus invited us to do, we will be in line with the Will of God, experience much greater joys, a sustaining peace, and be able to serve and care for others more effectively as a natural (or supernatural) result.

Does putting the Kingdom of God second or third or fourth instead of first in our lives fall into the category of idol worship? Sometimes yes and sometimes no. That may be more of a semantics argument than a theological argument. Nevertheless, we all do fall short and sometimes miss the mark so drastically that the cares of this world, things such as jobs, money, possessions, opinions, and even religion, do become our idols. In these instances we are, in essence, worshiping them.

When this happens we are in trouble. We are lost. We began to care less about those around us and less about our relationship with God. As a consequence we are in danger of stumbling on our path and hurting ourselves and those around us.

The Golden Calf of politics is most often power, opinion, agenda and pride. It is often fueled by the brokenness in a person's own heart, mind and psyche. Psychological disabilities such as over-inflated ego, narcissism, and a variety of other issues can make a person much more susceptible to worshiping their own Golden Calf gods. When we worship these political mini-gods our own opinions can become daggers and our words ammunition with which we may seek to obliterate any dissenting voices or views. Left unchecked, we may attempt to bully, belittle and silence anyone who would seek to knock down our Golden Calf opinions.

In the current era of Twitter and other social media, this type of unhealthy behavior is at our very fingertips if we have been rendered weak enough to cave into its temptation.

You don't have to look too far into the political arenas to see this poisonous Golden Calf conduct. It is everywhere. As many have reported we are currently living in a political climate that has become much more polarized and tribal than at any point in decades. Sadly, people in both major political parties are making Golden Calf gods of their own opinions, policies, agendas, and winning at all costs. In these instances Jesus Christ has been pushed aside. And the Christ-like attributes of bearing no false witness, being loving and kind, keeping no record of wrongs, striving to be patient, refraining from braggadocious or boastful behavior, and living a life of integrity, dignity, and common decency are quite often nowhere to be found.

I genuinely implore all of those in every corner of each political party to look deeply into the mirror of self-reflection and contemplate this unfortunate reality.

It also grieves me greatly to see Evangelical leaders and their congregations giving a green light to political leaders who are engaging in Golden Calf idolatry. This is the very time when we as Christian leaders and Christians should be loudly and forcefully calling upon those in power to retain the values and virtues which we hold so dear such as dignity, mutual respect, thoughtfully listening to one another, patience and kindness as well as personal and professional integrity. These are the attributes of Jesus Christ and when they are brushed aside they clear a path for the Golden Calf to rear its ugly head.

This will always be a challenge for humanity. As it has always been a challenge of the human heart. Whether it was 2000 years ago, or whether it be 2000 years from now we will always struggle to stay on the path of keeping the Kingdom of God first and pushing our idols aside.

Even in the face of this Golden Calf disease so prevalent and systemic in our society I remain hopeful that in the end love will win. That hearts of good intention will prevail. For one who loves, who is others-centered and filled with decency, dignity and integrity, has already won.

I sincerely hope and pray that some of my fellow Christians who have lost their way will strive to get close to Jesus once again and let His great love and compassion search the depths of their hearts so that He may transform them and reclaim that which has been lost.

Yes, we are all prodigal sons and daughters from time to time. But let us hope that we too may come back home after having destroyed our Golden Calf idols so that once again our Father in heaven may have a great party of rejoicing in our return.

This is my hope, this is my prayer.

I love the words Dr. Martin Luther King Jr. shared during the height of the tumultuous Vietnam War and Civil Rights era. I think his same sentiment could be echoed today: *"there is a cancer in the American spirit and what we need is a revolution of values, integrity and dignity."*

I agree.

We need to identify our Golden Calves and do away with them once and for all.

When we yield to any temptation we have made lust our God. Lust for power, lust for acceptance, lust for prestige, lust for control, lust for having our opinions accepted as fact and truth. Temptation, however, in and of itself is not a bad thing. At its best it can be used to reveal to us the part of our inner-self that needs a transformational healing.

Imposters

I used to play guitar and keyboards in rock and pop bands back in the day. Some of the clubs we would get booked in were pretty much dives, while others were actually relatively nice clubs. I remember one club we played in off and on for the better part of a year. There was this guy there, let's call him George. George was a friendly guy. Everyone in the band loved seeing him show up at the club. He had a friendly demeanor and was easy to talk to. He dressed well. He always wore an expensive suit and had a fancy watch. George seemed genuinely interested in each one of us in the band. He would always ask us what was going on in our lives, talk about music and seemed to enjoy chatting it up with us.

One thing I remember about George was that every night we played he would send up rounds of drinks for the band. That's right, every member of the band got his or her own drink and George would send them up all night long. It was obvious that George had a lot of money from the way he spoke, to the way he bought us drinks, to that expensive watch he wore.

I always liked him and appreciated the fact that he seemed to enjoy us so much. When our band finally ended its run at this particular club we said our cordial goodbyes parted ways with George.

I really didn't think about him again until a couple years later when I read his name in the newspaper and then saw him on the local TV news. It was then and there that I discovered George wasn't at all what he appeared to be - a successful businessman. At least not in the legitimate, legal sense of the word. In the news story they said that George had been arrested, sentenced, and put in prison for *counterfeiting money.* Evidently, when George was buying our band round after round of drinks night after night, he was passing along counterfeit twenty dollar bills. I guess maybe he really didn't like our band that much after all. He just needed to launder his money.

People aren't always what or who they claim to be.

There are some leaders in the Christian religion that indeed *look* the part. They wear the right clothes, speak in Christianese, have graduated from a well-respected seminary, can quote Bible verses, and maybe even have the perfect smile and a gift for preaching a rock-star sermon. However, if you examine some of the things they are saying a bit more closely you will often find that they are not representing the One they are claiming to represent - Jesus Christ.

All too often they are representing whatever agenda they may personally have or whatever political position they may hold. Sometimes these traits are hard to pick up on because they are cleverly disguised. Other times they are easy to spot.

This unfortunate reality has become highlighted in the Age of Trump as certain conservative Evangelicals have but one agenda: To prop up Donald Trump as some kind of a *savior* for their church's dogma and doctrine. We need to look deeply at these imposters and see them for what they are. They are counterfeiters just as much as my old friend George was. Only instead of passing along counterfeit twenties they are propagating counterfeit interpretations of scripture and passing it off as the Word of God.

We need to call them out and call them up to a higher standard. God's standard. And if they continue in preaching a counterfeit theology, their congregations need to consider getting up and leaving as fast as they can. Just as someone living in an abusive relationship needs to *get out now* and not come back unless the other person has been fully healed, so to must one *get out of an abusive church.*

There are plenty of Christian pastors around the country who are seeking first and foremost a relationship with Jesus Christ. Their preaching and teaching reflects that of Jesus. I want to make certain you know this. *There are great, loving pastors and congregations out there.* There *are* churches and congregations all around our country that are *filled with Grace.* But there are also a few bad apples spoiling the whole bunch. Hijacking Christianity. And some of them get a lot of media attention.

Jesus himself spoke of these imposters, these counterfeiters by saying, *"They come to you in sheep's clothing but inwardly they are ferocious wolves." (Matthew 7:15)*

As Christians it is imperative that we stay close to Jesus so that we may be able to better distinguish His voice from the voice of an

imposter.

Elvis, Vegas and Jesus

I was in Las Vegas a few years ago attending a broadcasters conference. While most of my Las Vegas time was spent at the convention center, I did get a chance to walk up and down the famed Vegas Strip a few times. If you have ever been to Las Vegas you know there are a lot of claims about Vegas that may or may not be true. The same can be said for what I am about to tell you.

My first night there, you won't believe this but, I saw Elvis. Yeah! Crazy, right? I saw Elvis Presley in Vegas. At least that's who the guy was *claiming* to be. He did look a lot like Elvis and he sounded a lot like Elvis too. I saw him on the Vegas strip right in front of a club called Margaritaville. He was pretty convincing. I skeptically and humorously thought to myself, "It's a miracle! Wow. *Elvis is alive* and singing on the streets of Vegas."

As I left Elvis and walked a little farther down the late night Vegas strip, standing right in front of the Flamingo Hotel - *I saw Elvis again!* How did he get here before me? How did he get here and change his clothes so quickly? Again, this guy was *claiming* to be Elvis. And again, he looked and sounded like the real deal but I couldn't help walking away slightly confused. Or maybe bemused.

The real kicker for me, the clincher and the "ah ha" moment, was when I arrived at the hotel-casino Ballys. It was another half-mile walk down the Vegas strip but *there was Elvis again!* He was in yet another outfit. This time I had my doubts because not only had he changed his outfit again, he had somehow managed to change his hairstyle and lose about 50 lbs. All in the last ten minutes. I didn't buy it. You can't pull one over on me. He may have been *claiming* to be Elvis, but this was not the real Elvis.

Sometimes things aren't what they *claim* to be.

Here's another Vegas claim.

Lucky 7, lucky 7! Everywhere I went in Vegas I saw a sign that read

"Lucky 7." I don't know why the number 7 is supposed to be so lucky but it is everywhere. It was in most all of the windows, on every sign and on most every slot machine. It was even in video poker games and on all of the gambling tables. I mean, everywhere I went there was something claiming to be *Lucky 7*.

I saw a lot of people gambling on Mr. Lucky 7. I even put a few bucks on Lucky just to test out his claim and I am here to tell you that Mr. Lucky 7 is not so lucky after all. I lost my money. All of it. He should really have called himself *unLucky 7*. He took $10 from me in less than 5 minutes. Yeah, I'm a big time gambler. Not.

There are those in Christianity who *claim* that Donald Trump was appointed by God.

Here is the truth: I don't know if he was appointed by God or not, *but neither do they.*

It is a false claim.

And a dangerous claim that is leading some people to worship him like an idol.

Like a Golden Calf idol.

Don't believe every claim.

Leaning Towards the Golden Calf

There are at least two main problems with the assertions of the conservative Evangelicals on the political right who are propping up Donald Trump as some kind of spiritual savior.

The first problem is the ignoring of dozens, if not hundreds, of actions, inactions, words, and lack of words conveyed by Donald Trump that have traditionally been deemed unworthy by most Evangelicals of Christian discipleship. We all say and do some wrong stuff but Donald Trump is a serial offender. Propping up - as some kind of Christian figurehead - a guy who is a repeat moral offender, who tramples on traditional Christian values daily without any trace of repentance, remorse or regret, is not only hypocrisy in its extreme it is also misleading, cult-like, and dangerous.

The other big problem is the casting of Donald Trump as some sort of heroic Biblical character, worshiping the man himself life a Golden Calf. Some on the right have cast him as King David or even as the second coming of Jesus himself. (I should also note that some on the left have cast him as Caesar or Pontius Pilate or even Judas.) Tempting as these type-casts may be, we in America want to stay far, far away from this kind of labeling with our elected officials as it has the possibility of leaning us towards a theocracy. The obvious problem with a theocracy is that no religious group, with all of its various factions, has ever been able come to a consensus on an interpretation of God, or if there even is a God. Holy wars can result from walking down this path and that is not where most of us desire to be. Separation of church and state is a powerful, protective and positive concept that must prevail for a democracy to stand. It is foundational for the good of all people and all religions.

These recent Biblical character parallels with politicians are false equivalencies that one should refrain from making. We do not want to worship the Golden Calf cult of Trump (or any other President) nor do we want to be sucked into worshiping our opinion that he is some type of Judas character.

Go, Sell Everything You Have...

There are many kinds of Golden Calf pitfalls in life. Listen to what Jesus tells a rich man longing to be His disciple:

> *"'One thing you lack,' he said. 'Go, sell everything you have and give to the poor, and you will have treasure in heaven.*

Then come, follow me.'" (Mark 10:21)

At first glance, this Bible passage makes us think about giving away all our money or selling all of our possessions. But taken in context with the Bible as a whole, it encompasses so much more. It should be noted that Jesus is *not* asking us to give away all of our money in this passage. No, instead, He is again making the point that we need to put Him, God, The Kingdom, first in our hearts - and all our other stuff second.

Often overlooked in this passage is that it's not just about "putting second" our *material* possessions. It is about giving up - or putting second - things that are sometimes much more difficult for us to let go of. Many of us often act as if we worship our own opinions. Are we willing to give up our opinions? Many of us become upset when someone has a differing point of view or tells us our point of view is wrong. Are we willing to let go of our need to be right all the time? Are we willing to let go of our anger and frustration? Are we able to give up our need to prove that we are correct and others are wrong? Are we willing to give up our right to ourselves? Indeed, sell all of *these things*, and take up your cross and follow me - says Jesus.

That's hard stuff.

In fact, it's impossible for us to do alone.

The good news is this: When we don't give up all of these things, because none of us can fully achieve this on our own, Jesus still loves us anyway. This is the heart of the Gospel. Grace. But as disciples we must strive, we must continue on a day-to-day, hour to hour and sometimes minute to minute basis to put Jesus *ahead* of our opinions, our agenda, our lust for power, our need to prove our political point, our need to be the one who always wins the argument.

This is the setting aside of all our golden calves and walking with

Jesus Christ. It is Christian belief that it is impossible for any human to achieve this alone. But with God, with Jesus and with God's Spirit living inside of us, all things are possible.

Letter to Hijackers

Please stop chasing people away from Jesus! Please stop preaching unloving politics from your pulpit. God wants you to look in the mirror and wants to help fix *you*. And God wants to help fix *me*. God does *not* want us to throw stones of judgement at others. Be discerning, yes. Throw stones, no. Every time we do this, the throwing stones thing, we are pounding yet another stake into the wrist of Jesus Christ on the cross. The very One we purport to follow. Yes, in doing this we are crucifying Him all over again.

Jesus is about the *individual*. His message is for you. His message is for me. He is not focused on any government or country. He is not focused on any corporation or institution. His focus was and is always on the heart, mind and soul of the individual. That is where He lives. That is where His Church resides. That is where His Kingdom is built. Not inside the four walls of a church building. Not in a particular town or city. Not behind the borders of a country. But in your heart and in my heart.

God is longing to break through and work on and in each of us. Christians, God is dying for us to learn to love *all* people. To *be* love for all people. This is how we witness. I know this is a hard thing to do as it demands we stop worshiping our opinions, our ideals and even our theology. We instead worship God. This allows God to work in us, on us and through us. Being a true disciple of Christ asks us to give up all that other crap. To put it all second and to put God first.

If you are still reading and not getting too mad at me for reminding you of this, then there is great hope for you - just as there is great hope for me.

It's really not that complicated.

Love one another. Sincerely, A follower of Jesus.

Appointed By God

"For false messiahs and false prophets will appear and perform signs and wonders to deceive, if possible, even the elect. So be on your guard; I have told you everything ahead of time." - Jesus

Is it possible for Christians to be fooled by false prophets?

Yes, absolutely.

As Christians we must always proceed with our spiritual eyes wide open and be wary of those who would utilize small sections of the Bible to support their agenda while neglecting the whole. Cherry-picking the Bible - taking passages out of context - is not of God. When confronted with a potential false teacher we must always ask ourselves these simple, fundamental questions: Are their practices meant to glorify God, or themselves? Are their teachings meant to lead us toward glorifying God and the loving of all people, or are they trying to get us to accept a particular exclusive agenda or opinion? Are they perfectly clear that salvation is a free gift of Grace, or does their preaching and teaching have a to-do list - a list of things that you must or must not do in order to get into heaven?

Entering the Danger Zone

One of the most dangerous and disturbing claims that has been made or implied by many conservative Evangelicals is that God somehow had a hand in Donald Trump becoming president of the United States.

First of all, this is a ridiculous claim because no person on earth knows the detailed mind of God.

One could make an argument that God possibly had a hand in the election of Donald Trump. But in doing so one would then need to concur that God has a hand in getting every president of the United States elected. To single out Trump without including all others is not only ludicrous, it is a grievous manipulation of the Christian flock.

Trump's campaign manager, Brad Parscale, implied or cleverly flirted with the idea that Trump was sent by God to save the country when he wrote on Twitter, *"Only God could deliver such a savior to our nation."*

Even Secretary of State Mike Pompeo stated, *"Could it be that President Trump right now has been sort of raised for such a time as this, just like Queen Esther, to help save the Jewish people from the Iranian menace?"** Those of us who are long time Bible readers and students of Christianity are well aware of the Christian dog whistles being blown here.

---

* Mike Pompeo, stated, *"Could it be that President Trump right now has been sort of raised for such a time as this, just like Queen Esther"*
https://www.washingtonpost.com/world/2019/11/01/trump-administrations-obsession-with-an-ancient-persian-emperor/

Citing a Biblical character or a Biblical story and making a false equivalence to current events, and using the term "raised" are all very clever ways of igniting the Christian right. They are also a Christian Hijack.

Some have tried to play both sides of the equation.

For instance Jerry Falwell Jr., president of Liberty University, has stated, *"If you give God credit for a good president, then you've got to blame God when you have a bad one. So I don't think that's the way to look at it."** Most reasonable Americans would probably agree with the plausibility of this logic. However, at the same time, after Falwell endorsed Trump in 2016 he also said, *"God called King David a man after God's own heart even though he was an adulterer and a murderer."* This was obviously stated to try to rationalize Donald Trump's immoral behaviors. Falwell continued, *"You have to choose the leader that would make the best king or president and not necessarily someone who would be a good pastor."* Another cop-out. While not strictly stating Trump to have been appointed by God, in drawing the King David parallel in the first part of that statement, Falwell certainly seems to be implying that Trump is somehow on par with him - a Biblical character.

And there's more.

White House press secretary Sarah Huckabee Sanders said in an interview with the Christian Broadcasting Network News, *"I think God calls all of us to fill different roles at different times, and I think that he wanted Donald Trump to become president."**

These are troubling if not dangerous assertions, folks. Stating or implying that a leader of a country is somehow a God-appointed savior is how Holy Wars get started.

* Statement by Jerry Falwell Jr. : *"If you give God credit for a good president"* https://www.politico.com/story/2019/04/30/donald-trump-evangelicals-god-1294578

* Statement by Sarah Huckabee Sanders: *"...and I think that he wanted Donald Trump to become president."* https://www.cnn.com/2019/01/30/politics/sarah-

sanders-god-trump/index.html

However, bringing the sacred into politics is a great way to divide a country, if that is one's intent.

The disciples walked with Jesus in the flesh for three years and *still* did not know what He was truly up to. Saying that any one person is appointed by God is utterly ridiculous unless, of course, you say that all people are appointed by God for God's purpose. And stating that a person is appointed by God because they going to do God's will by furthering a particular political agenda, especially if you are in a position of church leadership, is not only ridiculous, it is manipulative.

The great majority of our lives will be spent not knowing or understanding the particular details of God's great purpose. We simply need to come close to Jesus, have faith, trust, believe and obey. God's will be done.

Jesus and Government

Jesus is not interested in nor is He focused on the overthrowing of a government but rather on the "overthrowing" of sin in a person's heart. He is not focused on the transformation of a political agenda nor any particular society, but instead on the transformation of the human soul. Indeed, Jesus is focused on the healing of the individual, not the collective. The collective, a government and a society, can and will only be transformed and healed when the individual's heart, mind and spirit are so transformed and healed. Not the other way around.

Indeed, the hypocrisy and the doublespeak of some Christians and Christian leaders has been astonishing in the Age of Trump. Let's take a moment and shine a light on a couple of ancient scriptures and how they might relate to this hypocrisy.

Look at this passage in 1 Corinthians. In the Apostle Paul's letter to the Corinthians he composes one of the most beautiful and concise definitions of Jesus Christ's love ever written.

> *"Love is patient, love is kind. It does not envy, it does not boast, it is not proud. It does not dishonor others, it is not self-seeking, it is not easily angered, it keeps no record of wrongs. Love does not delight in evil but rejoices with the truth. It always protects, always trusts, always hopes, always perseveres." (1 Corinthians, 13:4-7)*

Now let us examine a few of these love attributes and descriptors in relation to Donald Trump's behaviors.

Does Trump exude patience? His erratic and spontaneous tweeting about any given issue of the day, at any time of the day or night, suggest the answer is no. He is not patient.

How about Kindness? Would you say that Trump exhibits kindness? The answer here is clear: no. He does not. He has thrown many, many people under the bus for challenging him. He throws insults around like a misbehaving child. Remember his name-calling: "Little Marco" and "Cryin' Chuck Schumer," or "Shifty Schiff," or how about "Sleepy Joe," or calling Mika Brzezinski "dumb as a rock" and "low I.Q." And now that the 2020 presidential campaign is in full swing he has added, "Mini Mike." There are literally hundreds of examples of Donald Trump being not just unkind but acting flat out rude towards other people.

Does he ever envy? Hard to read his mind on this one. Although the way he talked about the crowd size at his inauguration in comparison to the crowd size at Barack Obama's inauguration (along with other size comparisons) one might be able to build a case that he is envious of Barack Obama. But again, hard to read this one and I am not a psychologist so I'll just stick to provable, factual stuff. Speaking of that....

Does he engage in boasting? I'll let you discern for yourself. Here are just a few of his quotes: "No one respects women more than me. No one reads the Bible more than me." "Nobody knows more about taxes than me, maybe in the history of the world." "Nobody's ever been more successful than me." "Nobody is better on humility than me." "I can be more presidential than anybody. I would say more presidential, and I've said this a couple of times, more presidential other than the great Abe Lincoln." "I am the chosen one." ...Again I'll ask, does Trump engage in boasting? Yup.

Does Donald Trump dishonor others? In a word, yes. Here is a quote from Donald Trump on women: "I just start kissing them. It's like a magnet. Just kiss. I don't even wait. And when you're a star, they let you do it. You can do anything. Grab them by the pussy. You can do anything." Here is Trump dishonoring Former Florida Governor Jeb Bush: "lightweight" "desperate and sad" "a pathetic figure" "low energy individual" "a loser" "dumb as a rock" "puppet." Here's yet another one where he even dishonored actor Robert De Niro, calling him "a very low IQ individual." I could literally fill up an entire book with his dishonorable statements.

Is he self-seeking? Sure seems like it. Although we cannot know Trump's deepest motives he certainly acts and reacts in such a way that is much more self-centered than others-centered.

Does he keep a record of wrongs? There have been numerous times when people have challenged or criticized him and he has in turn parted ways with them to put it nicely. Throwing them under the bus might be more accurate. So yes, he keeps a record of wrongs, holds grudges and acts upon those grudges when possible.

Does he delight in evil? Remember Charlottesville? Remember the torches and the neo-Nazis and White Supremacists chanting, "Blood and soil," "White lives matter" and "You will not replace us"? Remember when Donald Trump called those neo-Nazis and White Supremacists "very fine people?" The question is, of course, why doesn't Donald Trump immediately call out and emphatically condemn neo-Nazis and White Supremacists when they are spreading hate and racism like this? Both are by definition hate groups and both are arguably being driven by evil forces. While I don't think you can make a definitive case that Donald Trump was *delighting* in this evil, he sure wasn't condemning it. In addition, when Donald Trump and his administration have locked up parents and their children and separated families at the Mexican border, they have said that this action would act as a "deterrent" to keep other people from coming into our country. That's not a moral reason for locking people up. Whether this action may or may not be a deterrent has yet to be proven but separating kids from parents when no law has been broken (many refugees were seeking asylum) or engaging in mass incarceration without proper food, medicine or psychological care is certainly not a loving thing to do. It is not a Jesus thing to do. I would go one step further and say that it either touches upon evil or the very least it is quite simply an inhumane way to treat people. Which I guess could be called evil. It's not much of a stretch to say that while Trump may not *delight* in evil he certainly is willing to use its manifestation for his political purposes.

Does he rejoice in truth? No. Absolutely not. This has unfortunately been proven over and over again. He calls the truth lies and calls lies truth. According to the Washington Post's Fact Checker database, as of this writing Donald Trump has said or tweeted over 16,000 false or misleading claims since he has been in office.

The evidence of Donald Trump's amoral behavior with regard to the Apostle Paul's description of love in the Corinthians passage is without question overwhelming. But the most troubling aspect of all is the deafening silence among certain Evangelical supporters of his when he says these things. Especially when they have used these identical behaviors as a moral benchmark for others.

Some Christians will argue that they don't want to have a

president that is all lovey-dovey. That they don't want a leader of the free world who is kind and patient and who keeps no record of wrongs. They instead want someone who is tough and strong, cruel and crass, someone who can easily bomb the enemy if need be. If that's what they desire, that is their prerogative. But don't equate an immoral leader with Jesus Christ or the preferred attributes of Christianity.

I would assert that no one has ever walked the face of the earth who was stronger or tougher than Jesus Christ, and He didn't have to be an asshole to be that way.

His strength and toughness were that of perfect moral character and impeccable personal integrity. Jesus was strong enough to turn the other cheek. Strong enough to resist temptation. Tough enough to be a servant to the most vulnerable, the ones who could not repay Him. Tough enough to take on the sin of the entire world and let Himself be humiliated by being crucified on a cross.

That is a tough and strong leader. One who does not lead by force or coercion but by influencing others through loving them unconditionally, serving them completely, and laying down their life and all of the riches and power they could have possessed, for the sake of others. Of course no human will ever be what Jesus Christ was when He walked the earth but His attributes are certainly something each one of us should strive for and aspire to.

There are certain Christian leaders who will cite as an excuse for not criticizing Trump's behavior or policies a passage from the Bible which states, *"All of you must obey those who rule over you. There are no authorities except the ones God has chosen. Those who now rule have been chosen by God." (Romans 13:1)* But they ignore the numerous Biblical examples of prophets who spoke truth to power. John the Baptist was beheaded because he confronted an unjust ruler. Jesus was crucified because he refused to bow down to Rome. And most certainly Paul's passage in Romans isn't suggesting that God chose Hitler or any of the other ruthless, murdering dictators throughout history.

And if one needs further clarification on our speaking truth to corrupt power one need look no further than Matthew 25: 31-46, the parable where Jesus says that people would be judged by how they treated the poor, the hungry and the stranger. Most certainly these words of Jesus need to be taken into account if one's government is neglecting or mistreating such people.

As I've stated before, *cherry-picking Bible passages to support one's stance without considering the Bible as a whole is bad theology.*

Nonsensical Assertions

It is the right of every person in this country to choose an immoral leader if they so desire. But it is an utter falsehood to claim that a lying immoral offender has been appointed by God. It is also absolutely unprovable, therefore can only be described as a propaganda tool being used by some to manipulate the thoughts of others.

In the religion of Christianity, God sent Jesus Christ whose sword was His Word and His love, hope, peace and forgiveness the fruits of His labor. He did no doubling down on falsehoods (He never made them) nor recklessly and relentlessly retaliated against those who disagreed with Him.

Again, if you want a president to behave in a childish manner contrary to the Life of Jesus, that is fine. But do not claim this person to be appointed by the Almighty. Do not claim Trump to be the savior of Christianity. He is not. If you are a Christian or Christian leader who supports him then by all means *do* call him out when he acts in immoral ways. *Do* call him out when he is lacking in integrity or behaving in ways that are obviously against the loving will of the Almighty. Maybe he will listen. Maybe he will repent and change.

We know the will of God. It is really quite simple. The will of God is *that we love one another.*

Religious leaders and fellow Christians, when Donald Trump blatantly comports himself in a way contradictory to that of our Lord, call him out. And then *call him up to a higher standard.*

United States of Theocracy?

In 2019 as a guest on the TV show "Fox & Friends," Robert Jeffress said, "to resist government is to resist God himself."

Let me repeat that. In 2019 as a guest on Fox & Friends, Dallas megachurch Pastor, Fox News contributor and Trump advisor Robert Jeffress said, *"to resist government is to resist God himself."*

Let there be no doubt, Jeffress was *cherry-picking* one particular passage in the Bible *(Romans 13:1)* and using it to garner or shore up support for his favorite politician.

I've said this before but I'll say it again - only this time with gusto: *This Robert Jeffress assertion is not taking into account the Bible as a whole, and is therefore Biblically incorrect!* It is a dangerous point of view for anyone to have!

Some Evangelical Christian leaders today are acting as if they would actually like the USA to be a theocracy. One of the fundamental problems with a theocracy is that someone must decide whose version or interpretation of God becomes the law of the land.

And who will that person be?

Every major religion, whether it is Christianity, Judaism, Islam, Hinduism, Buddhism or whatever, has underneath their religious umbrella many, many different interpretations of their theology. Consequently, each has multiple sects within their religion. Those sects were formed out of theological disagreement or geographical differences or a multitude of other reasons. Sometimes, even today, these sects argue amongst themselves. Throughout history some of these sects have even warred against one another. Do you see where I'm going with this?

This is just one of the many problems with a theocracy. Whose interpretation of theology gets to be the law of the land, is the question. Yours or mine? And what about those people who don't believe in your religion at all and resist? What are you going to do if they don't obey your religious law? Imprison them? Kill them? Doesn't sound very Christ-like, does it? The unfortunate inevitability of humanity is that all too often it has resorted to violence to resolve its disputes. The talk of having a theocracy, or even leaning in that direction, is misguided and dangerous.

Obviously, every leader in every religion on earth thinks that their interpretation of God is correct. Atheists and agnostics, too, think that they are correct. Even the apathetic and unengaged think they are correct. Otherwise they would move on to another belief system.

Evangelical leaders who are leaning in towards a theocracy and an authoritarian type government need to *get woke*. It is a really bad system for countless people. And Jesus doesn't just love some people. Jesus loves all people.

Present in the Pass

It was my senior year of high school in the small town of Puyallup, Washington. One of the classes I was taking in order to avoid studying too much was a PE (Physical Education) assistant class. I was fairly athletic and playing sports with a bunch of sophomores and juniors sounded to me like about as much fun as could possibly be extracted from high school.

There was no co-ed PE back when I attended high school. I was the assistant in a class of all boys. One afternoon the class headed down to our school's football stadium, about a half-mile jog from the gymnasium. We were to divide into two teams and spend the hour playing American football. Plenty of the guys wanted to lead the team I would be playing on, but being in a position of at least some authority to do more or less whatever I wanted, I appointed myself coach and quarterback. (Ego, hormones and immaturity can be a sorry and selfish mix at seventeen.) When I told you I was fairly athletic, that much is true. I was not, however, a gifted quarterback. More on that later.

Before I go any further I need to explain that we did not have our PE classes on the stadium's main football field. That wasn't allowed. It needed to be kept pristine. Instead, we played our games at the end of the stadium in an "off field" grass plot that was surrounded by an eight foot tall, sturdy cyclone fence. (For those who don't know - a cyclone fence is made of chain linked steel wire held up by tall steel poles)

I can't remember who was winning or losing that day but I do remember one significant play our team ran. I was to have the ball hiked to me and one of our speedsters, a junior named Jimmy, was to run a post pattern toward the end zone where if all went according to plan, he would catch the gently floating ball I had thrown and score a touchdown. That, at least, was the plan.

The ball was hiked. Sophomore and junior boys were flying all over the place and the pressure on me to release the ball was intense. Just in the nick of time I threw the ball with all my might in the general direction of Jimmy who was running as fast and as hard as I'd ever seen him run. With his blind determination and my imagined expertise in quarterbacking, victory, I was convinced, was at hand.

As soon as the ball left my fingertips, I could tell I had gotten off a pretty good throw. It was a perfect spiral. Up, up, and up some more. In fact, it was going a little higher and farther than I thought I was capable of. Then I saw Jimmy, running, running, jumping, up, up, up, and then suddenly a voice went off in my brain like an intense clap of thunder. "Nooooo!"

Just as Jimmy's hands touched the ball he quite unfortunately did a full face plant into one of the thick, steel poles holding up the cyclone fence. He hit the tall fence full throttle. It was a perfect face plant. Right between the eyes. He was down and out. There was blood coming from his lips and forehead and you could see the swelling of his nose already starting to rise. Everything on his face seemed to be bleeding, growing and changing color with each passing second. (As a side note, he did catch the ball, hung onto it and scored a touchdown!)

How could something so noble have gone so awry? I kept saying, I'm sorry, I'm sorry, but it didn't stop the bleeding, the pain or reverse the damage. Well, Jimmy was in pain for a while but within a couple of weeks he had made a full recovery and was fine. Whew!

Sometimes in life we are not so lucky. Malicious "quarterbacks" (false prophets) can lead us astray and into disastrous decisions, the ramifications of which can hold lifelong, painful consequences.

Sometimes we think we are doing the right thing by listening to and following them. We keep our eyes fiercely focused "on the ball" only to find the painful truth that we have been led into a fence. Or a metaphorical brick wall.

We need to be able to discern the voices of Truth from the voices of ill intent. There are a lot of people out there, some of whom are Christian leaders, who are throwing misleading passes for us to follow and catch. They would have us believe that somehow they are the only ones who can lead us to the Promised Land.

The only sure way to avoid disaster is learn to recognize the good voice of Truth. Jesus said, *"My sheep listen to my voice; I know them, and they follow me." (John 10:27)*

I cannot stress enough that the best way to recognize these faulty teachers is to learn to recognize the voice of the one True Teacher - Jesus. And how do we learn to recognize the voice of Jesus? There is only one way. It is the same way we learn to recognize the sounds, the inflections and the intent of a loved one or close friend.

We spend lots of time with them.

Listening.

Yet More Faulty Teaching

Here's another crazy quote from Pastor Robert Jeffress from 2017:

> *"In the case of North Korea, God has given Trump authority to take out Kim Jong-Un."*

Holy bullshit, Batman!

God does not want war or violence.

People wage war and commit acts of violence when they have failed at peace.

And God wants peace.

Indeed, we live in a fallen world full of flawed humans and evil. Sometimes, as a last resort, flawed humans engage in war as a way to protect themselves. Sometimes they justify their actions as being God's will.

Let me assure you that, in the religion of Christianity, war and violence are *never* God's will. Sure, there was some violent stuff in the Bible's *Old Testament,* but Jesus put an end to that. We are part of the *New Testament* now. New Life. New Wine. Jesus said, *"And no one pours new wine into old wineskins. Otherwise, the wine will burst the skins, and both the wine and the wineskins will be ruined. No, they pour new wine into new wineskins."* (Mark 2:22)

Justifying war as a Christian is like putting the New Testament wine (Jesus) into an Old Testament wineskin: it bursts apart. All is ruined. Jesus's teachings are ruined. Christianity is hijacked, spilling out wine like blood all over the countryside. Jesus does not condone war nor violence. Resorting to war and violence is simply the act of humans who have failed at peace. Yes, sometimes we war. Sometimes we humans use it as a last resort to stop evil. But more often than not, war is the end-result of humans failing to love one another.

Believing such propaganda as *"God has given Trump authority to take out Kim Jong-Un"* is believing faulty theology. Christian leaders who preach such things are unequivocally hijacking Christianity. Sadly, Christians who follow and believe such false teachings will end up sick in spirit, diseased at heart with a spiritual illness in their soul.

We must avoid the temptation to follow such teachings, even if we feel good and justified, for they will only lead us down an unhealthy path.

Again, so that there is no question about my assertions, let me reiterate my appreciation for the separation of church and state. A government and its people may indeed be driven into battle in self-defense from time to time. I am greatly thankful and indebted to all of those who bravely serve in the armed forces. War unfortunately happens in a fallen humanity. But war is never the will of Jesus Christ. To make such a claim is anti-Jesus.

Pizza, Pop-Tarts and Pepsi

I was still single. I was still young. I was sharing a house with two guys named Joey and Mike in Auburn, Washington. I was about 23 years old but still learning how to be an adult. (Actually, I'm still learning, but at that time I was kind of a "toddler" in my adulthood whereas now I may have graduated to the more advanced adolescence of my adulthood.)

One of the symptoms of my young-adulthood was that I was always trying out new things in a bit of a reckless way - and falling down on my metaphorical face much of the time.

I remember how my housemates and I thought it was silly and a waste of time and energy to take out the garbage every day. So instead of performing that daily task we brilliantly decided to bring a great big aluminum garbage can right into our kitchen and park it there. This made perfect sense to us. We could simply deposit our trash into the large can that was sitting in the middle of our kitchen, saving all that wasted time and energy of walking twenty feet outside to where the garbage can normally sat.

It only took us about three days to start questioning the wisdom of our choice. Do you have any idea how much three-day-old garbage can start to smell up a warm house? We held out for seven days and then we took the garbage can back outside where it stayed for good.

Another brilliant idea I had at the time was that I choose to eat and drink whatever I wanted. Not food that was actually good for me but rather food that *tasted* good to me.

One of my standard breakfast routines was to pry a piece or two of cold, leftover pizza off of the countertop, eat it, and then follow it up with a box of Pop-Tarts. Yeah, that's right. I would eat all of the Pop-Tarts in the box washing them down with my favorite morning drink, a can of Pepsi Cola.

Warning: Do not try this diet at home.

In order for me to keep up this very unhealthy breakfast routine I had to carry around a bottle of Maalox (an antacid). I kept it with me at all times. And a single dose would not suffice. Most often I would need to take a big, long swig of Maalox straight out of the bottle to calm my upset stomach. Yeah, I was making myself very sick with my unhealthy diet.

Again, do not try this diet at home.

Thank the Lord it was at about that time in my life that I met this cute little brown-haired girl. She quickly sensed the error of my ways and made it her mission to change some of my eating choices. One of the first gifts I ever received from her was a great big basket filled with healthy fruits and vegetables. That cute little brown-haired girl would later become my wife. Let me rephrase that: The cute little brown-haired girl who started me on a healthy path in life would later become my gorgeous, smart, wise, fun, creative, best-friend, everything-partner and always amazing wife.

There are so many paths we can take in life. So many choices. Some of them are good while others can really mess us up.

In a recent sermon Evangelical Christian Pastor Jim Bakker told his followers that if Trump doesn't get elected in 2020, *"leaders of the gospel and the political conservative leaders are going to be murdered."*

Sigh.

No, Jim.

That's just not true the way you've framed it. And please stop using fear as a weapon. That is not something Jesus condones. At all.

We can choose to believe the Jim Bakkers of the world or we can choose a more healthy spiritual diet. Jim Bakker's words may taste good to us, depending on our politics, but they are junk food. They will make us sick.

Our spiritual, emotional and psychological health is just like our physical health in the sense that, if we consume too much faulty information from our leaders or guides, we will pay the price. We will get sick. And so will those around us.

The World is Watching

There is a bad representation of Jesus being projected into the world by some right-wing Evangelicals. I feel sad and disappointed and sometimes frustrated and angry to have to write these words in order to help clarify who Jesus is and who Jesus is not.

Certainly these educated Christian leaders and pastors know better than this. Sadly, their "knowing better" makes their misleading statements all the more disturbing. That they would understand, at least intellectually, who Jesus is and yet turn their back on Him by not calling out the inappropriate behavior of the politician they promote from their podiums is disheartening enough. But when they go one step further and project to the world an image of a Jesus who is pro-belittlement, pro-rudeness, and pro-misleading people with falsehoods and lies, it's about as sad as it gets.

Those Christian leaders who support Donald Trump must *not* be silent on these things. They can support his policies if they like, but they need to come out strongly against his disturbing language, against the adolescent behavior, and send a strong message in no uncertain terms that this is not who Jesus is nor is it who Jesus has called us to be.

But instead of doing this, instead of standing up for and with Jesus, some have pointed to an Old Testament Biblical figure (King David) of questionable character who did great things and are comparing Donald Trump to him. (In the Bible, King David was a sinner whom God used for God's great purpose) This is a false equivalence and a textbook false moral equivalence.

Yes, Jesus loves all people including Donald Trump. But Jesus does not love the *actions* and the *words* of people who behave in such an astonishingly deliberate non-loving manner. Jesus also longs for His people to have a repentant attitude, an attitude of turning away from their destructive and immoral behaviors and turning towards Him, embracing His call for us to be loving, caring and kind. To live a life of compassion and humility. Donald Trump has not shown any signs of such repentance.

The bragging and boasting, the keeping records of wrongs, the misleading people and bearing false witness needs to be called out by his supporters. The Apostle Paul in his letter to the Galatians wrote: *"But the fruit of the Spirit is love, joy, peace, forbearance, kindness, goodness, faithfulness, gentleness and self-control."* *(Galatians 5: 22-23)* I ask my right-wing Evangelical Christian brothers and sisters: Is the one whom you strongly support, Donald Trump, exhibiting these traits? The obvious answer is "no."

Indeed, a Christian can love and support whatever politician they choose but they must speak out against serial misbehaviors of their leaders otherwise they are portraying Jesus to the world as condoning such things.

Porn Stars, Hush Money and Infidelity

Porn stars, Payoffs and Pussy-speak

I debated whether or not to write about porn stars, Donald Trump's infamous "pussy" statement and his alleged hush money payoff to Stormy Daniels.

I resolved to address it because the hypocrisy of some in the Evangelical community with regard to these matters is deeply troubling. But before we dive in, let's lay a little groundwork.

Are Christians hypocrites? Yes, of course we are. I would venture to say that every human being on the planet has been a hypocrite at one time or another.

A hypocrite is someone who claims to have moral standards or beliefs but whose behavior does not conform to these standards. A hypocrite is someone who does not "practice what they preach", who judges others for behavior they themselves engage in. A hypocrite claims to have virtue and piety but their actions belie their pretense.

Yup, I'm a hypocrite. Or at least I have been one from time to time in my lesser moments. That's yet another reason why I need a Savior. We all fall short in this way sometimes. Most of us who are healthy minded will upon reflection see how we have acted and take steps to improve ourselves. However, the hypocrisy with certain Evangelical leaders regarding porn stars, pussy grabbing and payoffs as they relate to Donald Trump is just remarkable.

My wish here is not to condemn porn stars. Nor is it to even condemn Donald Trump. It is simply to point out the double-speak some Christian leaders have been using these last few years.

To go from absolutely condemning pornography and porn stars from the pulpit to being unapologetically accepting and supporting of someone who has engaged in this behavior is doublespeak. To go from strongly condemning pussy-grabbing type actions and talk, from condemning the objectification of women and other forms of sordid sexual or predatory behavior from one's pulpits, to downplaying these things, brushing them under the rug, or simply saying you're giving someone a "mulligan" just because you support their political agenda is, well... utterly human, but certainly not of Christ. This is the definition of hypocrisy.

To speak of infidelity in marriage in such a way that one would think they are going to straight to hell if they were to partake in such an indiscretion and then to turn around and with loving arms claim it's suddenly not a big a deal when your candidate does it is both sleazy and, again, the definition of hypocrisy.

To be perfectly OK with someone using hush money to keep these indiscretions from becoming public is bad enough. But then to just sweep it all under the rug as if it was no big deal at all is in no way of Christ. Nor is it consistent with what certain conservative Evangelical pastors have been railing against from their pulpits for years on end.

To these Pastors and Christian leaders, I agree with Jesus and say, "hypocrites!" And maybe the very worst part of it is that in your hypocrisy you are leading others astray. You are confusing and misleading your congregations and ushering them *away* from Christ.

And the world watches.

And Christianity gets another black eye.

And Jesus is dishonored.

Jesus spoke very plainly about the hypocrisy of the Pharisees, the religious leaders of his day, and how wrong it was of them to act in such a way. It's startling how history is repeating itself in this manner. The parallels between many Evangelical leaders today and the hypocrisy of the Pharisees two thousand years ago is profound.

You could probably call their behavior today neo-Phariseeism.

Sadly, this blatant and ongoing hypocrisy is keeping many people from entering into a life with Jesus Christ. This is what grieves me the most. The spiritually-blind leading their flock - off a cliff.

I've said enough. You either get it or you don't. My message to these Evangelicals is first and foremost, stop it. Secondly, if you won't stop it, at the very least tell the world exactly what you are. Have the cahoonas to stand up and say you are hypocrites, going against your beliefs in quite a few areas for the purpose of achieving your own political goals. At least then you won't be lying.

A Note to all my Evangelical Brothers and Sisters

To all of my evangelical brothers and sisters who strongly support President Trump while brushing aside his moral failings as mere "mulligans": One of the great things about this country is that you can support and vote for whoever you want. You can vote

Republican or Democrat or for any other political party or candidate of your liking. You can even vote for Pee Wee Herman, Peter Pan or Mrs. Piggle-Wiggle if it suits your fancy. But if you support Donald Trump, you *must* call him out and hold him to the same standard of accountability and moral integrity that you have held others to for so long.

Why? Because when you don't, the list below is the impression non-believers both at home and abroad will have about Christians and Christianity. Worse yet, this is the impression they may have of Jesus Christ Himself.

- Christians are absolutely OK with serial lying when it suits their purpose or furthers their agenda. Lying doesn't matter if you are Christian. Not even if you lie 16,000 times in just a few years.

- Christians are OK with separating families and putting children in cages.

- A Christian is someone who thinks Jesus is an American.

- A Christian is someone who hates other religions so much they want to keep those religions out of their country by banning all those religion's followers from entering.

- Christians have no problem with someone sleeping with a porn star while already married.

- A Christian is OK with infidelity.

- A Christian is OK with rudeness, calling people names, and bragging and boasting about his or herself.

- A Christian likes to buddy up with his or her dictator friends. The kind of people that murder thousands of their own countrymen and women.

- A Christian is someone who breaks ties with friends and goes back on his or her word.

- A Christian is someone who bears false witness against anyone who speaks against them or challenges them.

- A Christian is someone who pays off other people in order to keep them quiet about embarrassing or illegal stuff.

- A Christian is someone who treats brown and black people differently than white people.

Still don't get it? Alright. Let the following list illustrate the severity of the hijacking of Christianity in the Age of Trump and strengthen my point that some conservative Evangelicals have lost their way. Imagine this (below) is the primary view non-Christians are having of Christianity based on the words, actions, silence and inactions of some Christian leaders in the Age of Trump.

- Jesus is absolutely OK with serial lying when it suits His purpose or furthers His agenda. Lying doesn't matter to Jesus. Not even if you lie 16,000 times in just a couple years.

- Jesus is OK with separating families and putting children in cages.

- Jesus is only an American.

- Jesus is someone who hates other religions so much that he wants to keep them out of His country by banning all those religion's followers from entering.

- Jesus has no problem with someone sleeping with a Porn Star while already married.

- Jesus is OK with infidelity.

- Jesus is OK with rudeness, calling people names, bragging and boasting about oneself.

- Jesus likes to buddy up with His dictator friends. He likes the behavior of people that murder thousands of their own countrymen and women.

- Jesus is someone who breaks ties with His friends and who goes back on His word.

- Jesus is someone who bears false witness against anyone who speaks against Him or challenges Him.

- Jesus is someone who pays off other people in order to keep them quiet about embarrassing or illegal stuff.

- Jesus is someone who treats brown and black people differently than white people.

Do you get it now? Do you feel the sting? Can you sense the absurdity? Are you deeply distressed by what some white Evangelical Christians and their leaders are saying?

Note to certain right-wing Evangelicals: You've lost your way. You've lost any moral authority you might have had. You sold it for someone who goes completely against many of the morals and values you have in the past, stated you hold so dearly.

It's time for you to have a true "come to Jesus" moment.

Tell me I'm wrong

Tell me that Jesus does not want us to be loving and kind and caring towards other people. Give me evidence that Jesus wants us to belittle and bully other people. Say to me that Jesus is happy that you are endorsing the actions and condoning the behavior of someone who tells falsehoods, lies and misleads the public again and again with misinformation. Tell me that you are ok with someone being cavalier about their numerous indiscretions.

Please submit your thesis, put forth your argument that these types of behaviors are what Jesus wants. Convince me that Jesus desires us to keep people from safety and to exclude people of different colors or different races or different religions from our - His - land. Please convince me that Jesus wants us to worship power and money and privilege and our own opinions. Please, Christian leaders, convince me of these things. I am willing to listen.

But you can't. Because to speak in such a way would be to go completely against the very God you purport to follow. It would be going against Jesus. The Jesus I know is not happy with these types of attitudes and the condoning of such unrepentant behavior. But I am listening if you would like to try to convince me otherwise.

The reality is we all make bad decisions. The question is, do we learn from our bad decisions? Can we make a turn in life, a change, choose a better direction?

We can.

With God's help.

Bad Decisions: The Wenatchee River

We were young. We were tough. We thought we were invincible. In reality we may have been all these things, but we also packed a healthy dose of youthful stupidity and naivety.

I was playing in a band named Heartbreaker. We were on the road doing a gig in Wenatchee, Washington. It was a beautiful, hot, early summer day and one of my band mates, Chris, and I were wasting our afternoon away by doing a bunch of nothing down by the Wenatchee river. The water was running high that day and the current was strong. But so were we.

I can't remember if it was a dare or just foolish youth that drove us to jump into that mountain river's icy rapids but somehow both Chris and I found ourselves quite literally up to our necks in the raging water's chill attempting to swim to the other side. Although both of us were really good swimmers, against the power of the current we struggled to make it across. It seemed like we were going to be in the unforgiving water's grip forever. It was far more difficult than we had calculated. But somehow, by luck or maybe by angels, we made it across.

Laying against the rocks on the far shore, both of us were completely spent. Our arms and legs dangled like rag dolls. Catching our breath, we suddenly realized that although we had made it across the river we now had to somehow swim back. It would be at least a ten mile hike through thick overgrowth in our bare feet to reach the nearest bridge and walk back across. That was when we made the second dumbest decision of the day. We decided to swim back.

This time every stroke was a defeating labor. There was no more toughness, no bravado, just two worn out young men wrestling with fatigue and the elements. And trying to stay alive.

To this day I really don't know how we did it but we eventually reached our home shore. By the time we made it back across, clinging to the rocks and branches of the shoreline and pulling ourselves to safety, we had drifted more than a half mile downstream. What a ride. We both swore that we would never, ever do that again.

I think about that day from time to time and realize just how lucky we were to have made it out if that river alive. There are undoubtedly a bunch of life metaphors in this story's experience but I'll leave it to you to sort them all out. What I want to say is this: There are forces in life that are deceptively powerful - and unforgiving. Whether we are contemplating swimming across a raging river or listening to a particular leader speak to us, we need to be smart, discerning, wise and cautious. Indeed, there are forces out there that can kill us - physically, mentally, emotionally and spiritually.

As is the thesis of this book, it is my contention that some in Evangelical Christian leadership have made bad decisions in putting politics over parish, power above people, and even their own agenda over Jesus. These bad decisions are misleading and are endangering others, damaging their relationship with Jesus Christ.

We need to be careful not to get sucked beneath the waters of their eloquent prose.

I pray every day these false teachers don't drag other people into the life threatening rapids with them. But if they do, I pray God's great wisdom, love and grace will hold and sustain those being pulled under until they are brought back to the safety of His loving shore.

Thoughts and Prayers

The Primary Purpose of Prayer

Yes, prayer can change things. But most often prayer changes us - then we change things.

Time and time again after yet another gun related shooting tragedy you will hear political pundits throwing out the phrase "thoughts and prayers." They will say something like, "Our thoughts and prayers are with the victims and families." It happens almost every time. Dozens of children get massacred by a gunman at a grade school and politicians' thoughts and prayers go out to the families. Dozens more are mowed down at a shopping center and again *thoughts and prayers* go out to the victims and their families. Again and again this is the response.

(Please note that I am not going to offer any policy ideas or opinions to the violence associated with guns that is ravaging America. You all have your own ideas. My intent here is to focus solely on prayer.)

Offering *thoughts and prayers* in and of itself is not a bad thing. Not at all. Those words can be quite comforting to the ones in pain. In fact, I think it is a wonderful thing to offer thoughts and prayers to those who are hurting, those in need, or those who have been wounded. However, we also need to remember the *primary purpose of prayer.*

The primary purpose of prayer is to have a relationship with God. As Jesus put it, to *become one with the Father as He is one with the Father. (paraphrased from John 17:21)* Prayer is also the primary work of any disciple of Jesus.

We need to know that God is not some giant genie in the sky who pops out of a heavenly bottle and answers our every whim or desire. While we are to make known our desires to God through prayer, the *primary purpose of prayer* is to have a *relationship with God.* To be in relationship with God so that God may do His/Her work in us and through us. Some call it being in communion or being one with God.

And through that relationship, that oneness, God will perform the great miracle of transforming our hearts and minds and, in doing so, mold and shape our thoughts and actions.

This is the primary miracle associated with praying. That God transforms our hearts and minds (this is God *in us*) and we in turn begin to look at and respond to the world differently. We begin to see life as God sees it, shaping our words and deeds to be more in line with God's great purpose. In other words, through prayer, *we* take action. Or maybe better stated, *God takes action through us.*

So while offering up thoughts and prayers is not a bad thing in and of itself, when the same politicians offer up *thoughts and prayers* again and again and again without any action, it makes one wonder if they are really doing the *work* of praying. And when they offer them up for the same circumstances (as we have witnessed many times after each mass shooting), without taking any real discernable action, you can almost guarantee that these words are either a simple human pleasantry or a political or religious stunt.

Why? Because if they were engaged in *the primary purpose of prayer,* sooner or later there would be a transformation of heart and mind which would lead to actionable change.

Don't let them hijack prayer. Enlighten them that the primary purpose of prayer. To hang out with God. Indeed, it is a relationship with God, being One with God, that transforms the heart and mind of the one praying, quite often leading to meaningful action.

The Metaphysical

While prayer transforms our hearts and minds in a truly miraculous way, I don't want you to think that God cannot also answer our prayer in a metaphysical way. Our Christian belief is that God can and does sometimes create a metaphysical miracle. That is to say, God causes something to happen in the physical world that is, as far as we know, humanly impossible. Beyond our understanding of the laws of physics.

There's a story in ancient scripture that illustrates these two distinct possibilities. The story goes like this: Jesus is out one day preaching and healing and hanging out with literally thousands of people who have come to hear him and see what He is all about. There are as many as five thousand men there that day, along with women and children. Some historians say there might have been as many as twenty thousand people who were there to hear and see Jesus.

Somewhere in that long day, Jesus's disciples inform him that they have a problem. All of these thousands of people are hungry and the disciples have no food with which to feed them. All they have for food is a couple fish and a few loaves of bread. Barely enough to feed a small handful of people let alone the thousands in the crowd.

So Jesus takes the fish and bread, says a prayer, and suddenly there is a bunch of food that arrives on the scene - miraculously. In fact, it's enough to feed everyone there and still have leftovers.

Whoa!

Is this a metaphysical miracle from God? Sure seems like it. Did hundreds of fish, hundreds of loaves of bread and maybe some pizza just suddenly start popping out of thin air? It's possible. It's not something any one of us can do and it sure goes against the laws of physics as we know them, but it's possible - a metaphysical miracle.

Let there be no doubt that God can do this kind of God stuff.

There's also another interesting possibility if you look a little deeper into this story. Many theologians and historians believe that a bunch of the people there that day may have been hiding food beneath their robes and their coats. Why were they hiding food? Because they were selfish and did not want to share. (Sounds a lot like people in this day and age, doesn't it?) But somehow, after Jesus began telling great stories and healing people, and when He prayed with but a couple fish and a few loaves in hand, suddenly *their hearts were transformed* from being selfish and self-centered into being selfless and others-centered. And they all began to share their food with one another. And because of this selfless act there was more than enough food to go around.

Cool.

Which of these two scenarios do you think is the greater miracle?

Is the greater miracle the possibility that fish and bread and pizza started popping out of thin air? That possibility is pretty freaking miraculous. Or is the greater miracle the possibility that thousands of *hearts* were miraculously transformed by spending time with Jesus? Transformed from being self-centered to being others-centered. From being selfish to being selfless. Consequently, beginning to share what they had with one another.

So which is the greater miracle?

A metaphysical miracle is absolutely astonishing, no doubt. But to me the transformation of a human heart which leads to action is a pretty awesome miracle itself. Indeed, it is one of the greatest miracles in life.

I don't have an answer for you as to which is the greater miracle or which actually happened on that day thousands of years ago. All I know is that through authentic prayer a human heart can be transformed, a mind can be changed, and this miracle can lead to new, life changing action, words and deeds.

With respect to the way the phrase *thoughts and prayers* has been used by some in the wake of all the gun related massacres in the US, I haven't yet seen any signs that the frequency and utter devastation of these tragedies has dissipated. I haven't witnessed a Biblical "fish popping out of mid-air" type miracle happening. I keep hoping. I keep waiting.

But I am also hoping that those offering up their thoughts and prayers after these and other types of tragedies will do the *work* of prayer. And that though the *work* of prayer they will develop a deeper relationship with God. A relationship that will cause a miraculous transformation of heart and mind that leads to meaningful action.

Authentic prayer changes us - and God, in us and through us, changes things. Let us all be open to God's great transformative power through prayer.

God Speaks

My daughter, Kelsey, one of my three young daughters, was about six years old at the time. Money was tight in those days so I was using our house as my office and our home phone for my business calls. Because young kids could be rather noisy at times my children were all well coached in the fine art and proper etiquette of "quieting down" when daddy got a business phone call.

We had a simple code worked out, a hand signal, for when those important calls came in. When I would answer a business call, if my daughters were playing nearby, I would gently but firmly raise my right hand up in the air and hold it there for a few seconds so they all could see *the signal*. It was meant to be a kind of stop sign. Usually my children would see my hand raise up and quietly proceed to another room to play.

On this particular day, however, our phone call etiquette would take on a whole new meaning.

A business call came in to me as all three daughters were happily playing in our main telephone room. (We didn't have cell phones back then. Just a phone attached to the wall with a long, curly cord. Yeah, I'm older than dirt.) The girls were fully engaged in their delightful songs and laughter but I still managed to gain their full attention when I raised my hand and gave them the "be quiet" signal.

Two of my daughters were immediately quiet and started to make their way out of the area but my third daughter, Kelsey, hesitated. It appeared that she was not too happy about having to leave the room right in the middle of her fun time and she was about to make her complete displeasure known.

I sensed this and raised my hand again and gave her a quick "no, no" shake of my head. This new action of mine did not seem to sit well with her either. She began speaking, "Daddy, I want to...," to which I swiftly raised my hand in a jolting fashion, scrunched my eyes, and mouthed-out to her my patented and emphatic "NO!" I tried to focus on the conversation with my business caller as I watched her then do one of those six-year-old, foot-stomp out of the room things.

But suddenly she turned back, stomping towards me again and began to argue her case further. "It's just not fair, we just..." she spoke and again I cut her off mid-sentence this time giving her a sharp raise of my hand and the meanest, maddest look I could silently contort my face into. I then pointed directly down the hall and mouthed the words "GO - NOW" as if she were now banished from my sight forever and sentenced to a lifetime of bedroom isolation as punishment.

Her lips pouted, her shoulders sank, and her chin fell to her chest as she begrudgingly left the room.

Maybe ten minutes later, as I was finishing up my business call, she came cautiously creeping around the hall corner and back into the room where I was standing. She then stood silently before me. I remember her lips were pressed tight together and she didn't say a word. She just held up a piece of notebook paper with some coloring on it and pointed it toward my face. I will never forget the picture she had drawn.

It was the face of a miserable looking man with blood-shot, angry eyes and steam shooting out of his ears. His face looked mean and evil, as if his whole head might explode obliterating anything and everything in sight. There was a name given to the evil man in her picture. It was written just underneath his hideous face. The name read "DADDY."

Ouch.

My daughter was sending me a message that I needed to hear. Although my daughter had to learn to respect the rules of our house, I needed to understand that she was only six years old and that she was far more important and precious than any business call would ever be.

Quite often God uses the people around us to send much needed powerful messages.

We can view our prayer life in much the same way. God desires to send us messages. And if we will be *still* and *quiet* enough in our minds to listen for those messages, our hearts will hear them. When we pray we are submitting our thoughts and requests to God. What we often neglect to do in our prayer life is to *listen*. To listen for the voice of God. As we listen, God begins to enlighten us to the realities of our being, our behaviors, the things in each of us that need to change - the things that need God's great transformative power. With God's Spirit living in our hearts, God will actually *be* the change we need. This is the oneness with God that Jesus was talking about.

Prayer is the door through which God can begin to do great work in us, on us and through us to affect the lives of those in our path.

Yes, our prayer life can have times of humiliation as we begin to realize, maybe for the first time, some of our flaws and woundedness. We see things that need to be healed. Difficult changes that need to be made. But along with that humiliation comes a great sense of joy, peace and gratitude.

Joy in knowing that our Creator loves us *anyway* and is doing a powerful work in us. Peace in the experience of being set free from the weight of the ties that bind. And gratitude that the One who loves us unconditionally is indeed with us and has transformed us for the better.

It is my hope that those who have been abusing Christ through their words, actions, silence and inactions will come to this place again. This place of deep authentic prayer. This place of Oneness. This place where Jesus can be the Light in the darkness and heal completely that which is wounded setting them back on the True path again.

That is my hope.

The Misuse of the term Grace

Christians believe that through Jesus Christ all are saved by Grace.

This was the primary purpose of Jesus Christ dying on the cross and rising from the dead. For those who may not know Jesus or anything about the Christian faith, the foundation of Christianity is that God sent his only Son Jesus Christ to die for us, and through His death and resurrection all are forgiven - we are all saved. It is finished. Once and for all. It's a done deal. We can do nothing to earn this salvation. It is a free gift to us from God. This, in essence, is Grace. This is the foundation of the Christian faith.

Having said that, there is this discipleship thing that comes along with grace. It is how we live out our day to day life with Jesus. And we can really screw it up. Screwing up doesn't alter our salvation but it sure can alter our lives here on earth. The assurance of being saved by Grace is not an excuse for bad behavior. Jesus calls us to discipleship, to high moral character, and to a life of love and integrity.

There is a beautiful summary of Grace that I have heard many times over the years and I'd like to share it with you. It goes like this:

Grace is the gift of pure, complete and unconditional love from God to us. It means there is nothing you can do to make God love you more, and there is nothing you can do to make God love you any less.

Up on a cross Jesus said, *"It is finished." (John 19:30)*

Indeed, it is done. If you screw up in this lifetime, you are forgiven. Got it? Your salvation is still assured. Amazingly, so is mine. But if you or I screw up badly in this lifetime, we will still pay a price here on Earth in one way or another. There is an earthly consequence.

I used to take a team of musicians to McNeil Island Federal Penitentiary and Washington State to do a music ministry. It was there that I met inmates who had committed horrific acts such as rape, murder and even mass murder. I might find it hard to forgive someone who had committed one of these acts against me or my loved ones. Yet through belief in Jesus Christ and His great gift of Grace, these inmates, even the ones that have committed the most heinous acts, are all forgiven and will spend eternity with our Lord.

Still, they have a price to pay here on Earth for their actions. Many of those I met need to be in prison for ten to twenty years and a few will be incarcerated for a lifetime. Some have extreme mental illnesses and can't control their violent behavior. Some have abused their rights, the rights of others, have taken the lives of innocents and continue to be a danger to society. Yet Jesus Christ *still* welcomes them back into His loving and forgiving arms through His infinite well of mercy and gift of Grace.

Having said all that, we do need to be careful when throwing around the term "Grace" when someone commits serial indiscretions, such as Donald Trump has for many years and in many ways. To say God's Grace has forgiven him for all of his indiscretions may be *spiritually* true but there is still a price that needs to be paid in this life. There are still consequences. So while Grace covers his eternal life, there are repercussions here in this world. There is still repentance (turning back to God) that needs to happen. There is still trust that needs to be rebuilt. And if Donald Trump or anyone continues to falter again and again as he most assuredly has, he is proving himself to be untrustworthy. When someone proves over and over again that they are untrustworthy we can easily discern that we must be more than cautious around those individuals.

Grace guarantees our salvation. Using it as a way to excuse bad behavior is a misuse of the term.

I recently watched an interview on TV with a handful of Christian women in Texas who were in essence wiping Donald Trump's slate clean, citing Grace. They were promoting the notion of him as a great president and were using Grace in such a way that projected the misnomer that all is forgotten, full trust is given, and that absolution had been granted *here in this life* - and that God was *just fine* with Donald Trump as he is now.

Why do I bring up the misuse of the word Grace by these Christian Texas women? Because the context in which these women used "Grace" is a hijacking of Christianity.

In light of Trump's continual non-Christian behavior such as lying, bullying and belittling people multiple times per day, I find these women's use of the word Grace to be cheap. And wrong. They made it seem as if his immoral behavior doesn't matter at all. His immoral behavior does matter. We have yet to see any evidence of a turning - of repentance. In fact, the evidence is quite the opposite.

The way these Christian women were using the term "Grace" in relation to Donald Trump is a misuse of the Grace of Christianity. They have cheapened it and in essence have hijacked God's great gift to further their political and religious agenda.

These women are *spiritually* correct that God forgives our indiscretions (yes, even Donald Trump's indiscretions and even mine), but putting a serial offender upon a Grace pedestal as if none of his bad behavior matters has cheapened the definition of

God's Grace and cheapened Christianity. It would have been better and more accurate for them to say that Donald Trump has made terrible personal mistakes and continues to act in a way that is not of Christ, but we love him, support him, and continue to pray that he will one day make a turn toward Jesus.

That would have been a factual and truthful statement for them to make.

Hope

Yet we continue to have great Hope. Even in the midst of Christianity's unfortunate hijacking in the Age of Trump.

> *"I remember my affliction and my wandering, the bitterness and the gall. I well remember them, and my soul is downcast within me. Yet this I call to mind and therefore I have hope: Because of the Lord's great love we are not consumed, for his compassions never fail. They are new every morning; great is your faithfulness. I say to myself, "The Lord is my portion; therefore I will wait for him." The Lord is good to those whose hope is in him, to the one who seeks him. It is good to wait quietly for the salvation of the Lord." (Lamentations 3:19-26)*

My wife and I have been married for over thirty years now. I won't give you the exact number because it makes me seem so freaking old. During our thirty-plus years together we have disagreed on countless issues numerous times. Sometimes our differences of opinion (and our momentary lapses of maturity) have led to arguments which have caused us to not speak with each other for a couple of hours. Yes, we have been so frustrated with each other in those lesser moments that it *feels* like we really don't like each other very much.

Indeed, we are human and act in immature ways sometimes. However, during our thirty-plus years together we have always held onto one thing: That our relationship was and is infinitely more important than our differences or our momentary "need" to be right. We understand somewhere down deep that you don't ever win an argument if you lose a relationship.

In those moments we have held tightly to the phrase, "God doesn't call us to like each other each and every moment but does call us to LOVE each other even when the 'like' part is bruised."

Love ain't easy, folks. And it can be doubly hard in those times when our negative emotions are lit up. Love is an actionable involving patience, kindness, letting go and *keeping no record of wrongs* (that one gets me every time).

I believe that the call for healthy human relationships far outweighs our differences of opinion. And that those who master the art of *relationship* will truly experience the deepest richness and abundance life has to offer. Those who do not develop this skill will have very few and often difficult or broken relationships.

This last political season has tested us all. It has strained our relationships as we have disagreed with so many of our family, friends and acquaintance's points of view. I have incredibly smart, educated and wise friends who have voted for and supported political candidates on opposite ends of the spectrum. I have unfortunately seen friends severely damage and even lose relationships altogether over differences of political opinion. This saddens me.

I have strong opinions and views about political issues myself. And I have had to stop myself from thinking at times about those with opposing opinions as... well... in the same negative way I'm sure they sometimes think of me.

Let us be passionate and stand up with all of our might for what we believe in, but let us never damage our bond with others. For after all, relationships with our family, friends and neighbors, and with our God are all we have.

Now is a sensitive time and there are unseen powers working to divide us. Let us disagree. Let us advocate for our beliefs. Let us stand and march and shout and cheer but let us never lose sight of our purpose in life: to love, help and serve others. Let our relationships not be hijacked by our differences in opinion during these tumultuous times.

Indeed, our walk with Jesus is about other people.

Let us love all people.

Guy in the Grocery Store Line

It was a couple days before Christmas. I was rushed. I was buying some last minute supplies down at the local grocery store. My hurry-up stress found me in one of those "I'm on a mission, I'm in a hurry, I don't care if it's Christmas time, get out of my way" kind of moods. With laser precision and lightning speed I mowed throw the aisles grabbing everything I needed. I was awesome.

Then came the dreaded checkout line.

Actually, I got lucky. It wasn't that bad. There was only one guy ahead of me. An elderly man who only had one item, so I figured he would be quick. But as I impatiently watched him I noticed that he was confused. First he tried to walk behind the register with the cashier. The cashier kindly pointed him back toward the aisle that he was to walk through.

He wasn't drunk. He just seemed disoriented. I noticed him desperately trying to understand what the cashier was saying. This elderly gentleman couldn't seem to figure out how to pay for his item. Finally, like he'd discovered money for the first time, he found his wallet. He fumbled around with his bills and change for a while and then paid.

After paying, he slowly turned from the checkout counter and walked off. The only problem was he walked off without his one item. After a few seconds passed the cashier grabbed this gentleman's forgotten bag and rushed it out to him just as he stepped outside the grocery store.

The cashier came back. Rang me up. I paid for my groceries and walked out to my car and started driving home.

But as I drove, I was really bothered. Not by the fact that this elderly man was slow or confused. No, that didn't bug me too much. What was bothering me was the fact that I did nothing to help this guy. I was right there. I was in the perfect position and yet I just stood there watching, doing nothing.

This all happened, as I said, a few days before Christmas. So I had to ask myself, "What is Christmas? Is Christmas just for *me*? Just some colored lights, a pretty tree, opening presents, a warm fire, good food, some sentimental songs and a candlelight church service? Am I - or am I not - living out the Gospel?"

In the Gospel we are called to be a witness to the Light – Jesus Christ. And one of the most powerful ways that we can witness is by serving and by helping others. In this one moment with the elderly man at the store, I had failed.

I don't want to let those opportunities that God places before me to slip by. I want to be a witness. I want to be a witness by loving and serving other people when the moments arise. When God engineers those moments, I want to let the Light of Christ shine in me and through me instead of hiding it or dousing out the flame.

God is providing opportunities for us to live out the Gospel each and every day. In small ways and in big ways, a few of which I have mentioned in this book. God is calling us to love and serve the immigrants. God is calling us to love and welcome those of different religions. God is calling us to love, serve and welcome those who do not look like us, those who may have different ways of identifying themselves than maybe we are familiar with. God is calling us to speak up and speak out against belittlement, bullying, bearing false witness, and idol worship. And to always seek to unite and be inclusive. God is calling us up to a higher standard. One of dignity, integrity, and high moral character.

As Christians we can lead or be led by fear - or faith.

Jesus has called us to faith, not fear. To be the Good Samaritan, not the racist traveler.

There are those on the religious right who appear to be so afraid of *the other* that they have succumbed to using fear instead of faith to lead their flocks. They are hijacking Christianity. They are hijacking hearts. They are infecting minds with their fear-based rhetoric. Pray for them.

Yet, there are also Christian leaders who are leading their flocks by faith, not fear. They are the ones preaching love for all and seeking to convey the heart of Jesus Christ.

Follow them.

The Quiet Servants - Following Jesus

It's sad that some Christian leaders today have forgotten the attributes of being a follower of Jesus. It's sad too that some have fallen into the trap of worshiping their own version of Christianity instead of worshiping God. And it is a shame when they drift towards using their platform to divide and exclude instead of fostering communities of unity and inclusiveness.

This book has attempted to shine a spotlight on some of their behaviors.

Let me be quick to say, however, that there are many, many healthy churches and great Christian leaders who are indeed following Jesus. I personally know some of them. Even now you can almost hear Jesus say to them, "Well done, good and faithful servants."

But for those leaders in and out of the church who have become confused, lost their way, and are now leading their sheep down dangerous paths, let this book be a reminder of Jesus Christ and His great message and example of love for all. Let us always seek to build our daily and lifelong walk upon Him and His values.

To love, to encourage, to greet one another in peace, to forgive, to always live and exude a life of compassionate humility, to be kind, to not provoke or slander, and to be hospitable to all people. These are the crystal clear attributes a follower must strive for.

Putting Jesus first in our daily lives will always bring forth an abundance of Living Water.

This Water will quench the thirst of a world in need.

Conclusion... Faith is Everything

There will come a time for us all.

A time when we will know, certain as the sun, that it is the end of our earthly journey.

None are spared.

No one will escape it.

The mortal grip of reality. That final place where only hope in the unseen is left. And we will grasp for it with all our might. You can count on it. It is the cold, sober truth that most of us simply lock away in a box stored somewhere in the deepest recesses of our minds. We don't want to think about it. But that box will one day be opened. There will be an end.

It may last a few years as we lie in some nursing facility unable to care for ourselves in even the most basic of ways. Where life has taken from us our ability to reason either through medication or dementia. Or it may last only a few minutes. As we lie on the floor, gasping for breath while a massive heart attack strips away all that we once thought was ours forever.

Then, all that we have here on Earth will be gone. Out of our reach. We can't move, we can't speak, we struggle for air... there are no options left. Not for any of us. Last call. Final curtain. Only Faith remains as we desperately cling to Hope.

It is at that point when we all will suddenly realize the incredible Truth: Faith is everything.

Oh, but to have experienced that wonderful reality sooner. To have not wasted so much time, so much of life on *stuff*. To have invested our days, our hours, our moments in growing our Faith garden by loving and caring and helping others and by just *being* with others, instead of acquiring *more*: more opinions, more absolutes, more false idols.

But here we are. The final stop. Attached to nothing. Now dressed in the warm blanket of letting go. Forgiving all, forgiving ourselves, being forgiven. What a wonderful comfort it is to have nothing - and yet have everything.

In the end there is nothing - nothing but Faith.

Faith is everything.

Start now.

Celebrate Life. Love and enjoy those around you. Help those in your path. Mend any broken relationships. Strive toward peace of mind, heart and spirit. Now is the time. Now is always the time. Life is short, fragile, wonderful, painful, beautiful and the most extraordinary miracle. It is a gift. Don't waste another second. Open the present. Be joy, life and a light for all to see.

A Note to my Atheist Friends

First of all, let me apologize.

I'm sorry that some religious people have let you down - or worse, hurt you. We know that all religions and all belief systems are flawed because they are run by people and all people are flawed. Sometimes flawed people hurt other people. Sometimes tremendously. And sometimes flawed people hurt other people using God's name.

Very little in life grieves me more.

I'm not going to suggest you go to a church. I would guess that's the last thing you need to hear. Nope, I'm going to mention something   different.

I'm just going to ask that you forgive us. Us Christians. The ones who have hurt or marginalized you using God's name. We shouldn't ever do that. Jesus would not do that nor does He want us to wound others like you.

Let me say as sincerely as I possibly can to all who have ever been hurt by the church or by ones using the Bible as a weapon - I'm truly sorry.

The Jesus I know loves you.

Unconditionally.

The Big Wooden Fork

"Thomas said to them, 'Unless I see the scars of the nails in his hands and put my finger on those scars and my hand in his side, I will not believe.'" (John 20:25)

It was one of those Big Sunday Dinners at my grandmother's house. The whole family was there. My mother, father, brother, sister and my cousins. I was barely knee-high to a caterpillar but could tell that all the food on the table was nothing less than a feast. There was steaming hot turkey and honey baked ham, beans with bacon, mashed potatoes and yams. There was an assortment of breads, rolls, sweets and pies. There were nut bowls, olives, chips and dips, there were fruit salads, egg salads and, my favorite, that special tossed salad with grandma's incredible homemade dressing on it. Those big Sunday dinners were legendary in our family and this one was nothing short of spectacular.

When the meal was over, the customary thing to do at my grandmother's house was to retreat into either the living room or the kitchen. Usually the women went into the kitchen to clean up the mess while the men, having already worked so hard at eating - or so they liked to say - would go into the living room to rest and relax. As a very young child I decided to follow the women into the kitchen, but before I left the table I wanted just one more taste of *grandma's incredible homemade salad dressing.*

So I climbed down off of my chair and secretly snuck around the table until I came upon the gigantic salad bowl. Then, while nobody was looking, I reached my small hand up over the side and carefully down into the bowl until I pulled out the big, wooden serving fork. It was just dripping with mouth-watering flavors. Mmmmm, it was soooo gooood. It had all of grandma's best herbs and spices mixed in and now they were cascading down the sensors of my palate. I was in heaven. With the giant wooden fork in my mouth I proceeded to prance my way into the kitchen.

Lost in my bliss, I was totally unaware of two things that were about to change my life. First of all, I was not aware of the many voices of wisdom and warning that had told me not to walk around with any sharp objects in my mouth. Secondly, I was also quite unaware of the protruding aluminum floor strip that separated my grandmother's dining room carpet from the kitchen floor.

Well, children being children, I didn't just trip and fall onto the floor. No, I fell *face first* onto the floor with the big wooden fork in my mouth. The delicious tasting salad fork had suddenly become a weapon of terror and pain as it lodged itself into the back of my throat. I'll spare you the gory details but I will say that in order to curtail the excessive bleeding, my parents and grandparents left the fork stuck in the back of my throat as they rushed me to the hospital.

To this day I never have figured out how the doctor got all those stitches way back in the deep recesses of my young throat.

The truth is... I don't really remember any of it.

You see, I was only three years old at the time and my earliest childhood memory is from about the age of four. But that's the story my family tells year after year, reunion after reunion. Sometimes though, even now, I will stand in front of the mirror with my mouth wide open and try to look in and see the scars. When I can't see them I will try to stick a finger or two back there to see if I can feel any scar tissue. I always start to gag before I can feel anything and consequently give up.

I guess the story's true. I mean, why would my family lie to me? Still, I would like to have some sort of proof. Like maybe a big ole scar on the side of my throat that I could wear as a badge of courage and honor for having gone through such an ordeal. Or maybe a picture of it or something.

"...and Thomas said to them, 'Unless I see...'"

I must be a lot like Jesus's disciple Thomas because sometimes I have all kinds of doubts about things I cannot prove. Even in my walk with Christ I sometimes have questions and doubts. There have been times in my life of personal pain where I'll find myself searching through Bible verses or scouring the pages of some old seminary book trying to find positive proof that everything about God is true. Where all the pieces of the puzzle fit together perfectly and logically. It's as if I'm saying "prove yourself to me, Jesus! Show me the scars. Let me touch you and *then* I'll believe. *Then* I'll know for sure you are who you say you are."

No, I can't actually see or touch the scars in my throat where the big wooden fork became lodged that day so long ago. But in another very real way I think I do see the scars. I see them in the strained agony I witness in my mother's eyes as she recounts the story of taking her small child to the hospital that day. I feel them in the pain I hear in her voice as she describes holding me close in her arms on that long and bloody ride to the emergency room. Yes, in a way, I do see the scars and I do touch the wounds and I *know* - for sure - that it really did happen.

"Then He said to Thomas, 'Put your finger here and look at my hands; then reach out your hand and put it in my side. Stop your doubting and believe!' Thomas answered him, 'My Lord and my God!' Jesus said to him, 'Do you believe because you see me? Blessed are those who believe without seeing me.'"
(John 20:27-29)

I believe Jesus Christ to be exactly who He says He is.

And I have great faith that even in this era of heightened hijacking of His name, Jesus lives and will live - forever and ever.

Amen.

Notes

All Biblical quotes are NRSV or NIV unless otherwise indicated.

All other quotes are multi-sourced from respected news organizations.

Chapter 1
"These aren't people, these are animals"
https://www.usatoday.com/story/news/politics/2018/05/16/trump-immigrants-animals-mexico-democrats-sanctuary-cities/617252002/

"Love your neighbor as yourself." - Jesus (Matthew 22:39)

Further reading on The Moral Majority:
https://www.britannica.com/topic/Moral-Majority

History of the Crusades: https://www.ancient.eu/Crusades/

Overview of the Inquisition:
https://www.history.com/topics/religion/inquisition

Overview of Constantine:
https://en.wikipedia.org/wiki/Constantine_the_Great_and_Christianity

Brief history of the Salem Witch Trials:
https://www.smithsonianmag.com/history/a-brief-history-of-the-salem-witch-trials-175162489/

The First Amendment of the United States Constitution:
https://www.law.cornell.edu/constitution/first_amendment

The Christian right:
https://en.wikipedia.org/wiki/Christian_right

Evangelicalism in the USA:
https://en.wikipedia.org/wiki/Evangelicalism_in_the_United_St
ates

*"Congress shall make no law respecting an establishment of
religion, or prohibiting the free exercise thereof..."* This, he said,
built a *"wall of separation of church and state"* along with Article
Six which specifies that, *"no religious Test shall ever be required
as a Qualification to any Office or public Trust under the United
States."* [Thomas Jefferson paraphrased]

Chapter 2
Quote from Donald Trump's Presidential Announcement Speech:
*"I would build a great wall, and nobody builds walls better than
me, believe me, and I'll build them very inexpensively. I will build
a great great wall on our southern border and I'll have Mexico
pay for that wall."* https://time.com/3923128/donald-trump-
announcement-speech/

Executive Order 13769:
https://www.whitehouse.gov/presidential-actions/executive-
order-protecting-nation-foreign-terrorist-entry-united-states/
A brief overview of Executive Order 13769.
https://en.wikipedia.org/wiki/Executive_Order_13769

Original statement pertaining to a Muslim Ban posted on Donald
Trump's Presidential Campaign Website:
https://www.cnbc.com/2017/05/08/trump-website-takes-down-
muslim-ban-statement-after-reporter-grills-spicer-in-
briefing.html

The original statement was subsequently removed from Trump's campaign website:
https://www.npr.org/2015/12/07/458836388/trump-calls-for-total-and-complete-shutdown-of-muslims-entering-u-s

Additional statements and tweets made by Donald Trump pertaining to a proposed Muslim Ban:
https://www.usatoday.com/story/news/politics/2018/04/24/travel-ban-donald-trump-campaign-promises-president-tweets/542504002/

Donald Trump's quote about defeating ISIS, "You have to take out their families."
https://www.cnn.com/2015/12/02/politics/donald-trump-terrorists-families/index.html

"You have to take out their families."
https://www.washingtonpost.com/news/worldviews/wp/2017/05/27/trump-said-he-would-take-out-the-families-of-isis-fighters-did-an-airstrike-in-syria-do-just-that/

https://www.nytimes.com/politics/first-draft/2015/12/02/donald-trump-says-terrorists-families-should-be-targets/?mtrref=www.google.com&gwh=72F59A1EE0ACED9DA72475616495B681&gwt=pay&assetType=REGIWALL

Chapter 3
The "Send her back" racist chant by Donald Trump supporters at one of his Rallies:
https://www.usatoday.com/story/news/politics/elections/2019/07/29/send-her-back-chants-trump-rally-open-wounds-greenville-nc/1828979001/

Donald Trump's "Go Back..." racist tweet.
https://www.usatoday.com/story/news/politics/2019/07/14/trump-tells-congresswomen-go-back-counties-they-

came/1728253001/
https://www.npr.org/2019/07/15/741827580/go-back-where-you-came-from-the-long-rhetorical-roots-of-trump-s-racist-tweets

Explanation, history and definition of a racist tropes in the United States:
https://en.wikipedia.org/wiki/Go_back_where_you_came_from

Neo Nazi and White Supremacists chant "Blood and soil" and other chants at a Unite the Right rally in Charlottesville, Virginia:
https://abcnews.go.com/US/happen-charlottesville-protest-anniversary-weekend/story?id=57107500

Donald Trump's insults of Mexicans and immigrants along the southern border of the United States:
https://time.com/4473972/donald-trump-&/

A brief history of Redlining in the United States:
https://en.wikipedia.org/wiki/Redlining

Current facts and statistics on Racial Disparity in the United States: https://www.sentencingproject.org/publications/un-report-on-racial-disparities/

"Send her back"
https://www.washingtonpost.com/powerpost/omar-trump-rally-with-send-her-back-chant-will-be-defining-moment-in-us-history/2019/07/25/acada110-aecd-11e9-bc5c-e73b603e7f38_story.html

https://www.nytimes.com/2019/07/20/us/politics/trump-send-her-back.html

Chapter 4
Dehumanization leads to ghettoization leads to extermination. The psychology of Cruelty:
https://www.npr.org/2011/03/29/134956180/criminals-see-

The Hijacking of Christianity in the Age of Trump

their-victims-as-less-than-human

Donald Trump's "Rat infested" quote:
https://www.cnbc.com/2019/07/27/trump-calls-baltimore-a-disgusting-rat-and-rodent-infested-mess-in-attack-on-rep-elijah-cummings.html

Donald Trump's "Shithole Countries" remarks:
https://www.cnn.com/2018/01/11/politics/immigrants-shithole-countries-trump/index.html

More on Franklin Graham's support of Donald Trump:
https://www.nytimes.com/2018/02/26/us/billy-graham-franklin-graham-trump.html

Trump's "Grab them by the pussy" comments:
http://www.slate.com/blogs/the_slatest/2016/10/07/donald_trump_2005_tape_i_grab_women_by_the_pussy.html

61 things Donald Trump has said about women:
https://theweek.com/articles/655770/61-things-donald-trump-said-about-women

"Somebody needs to read poor Greta Genesis, Chapter 9," Robert Jeffress: https://www.newsweek.com/robert-jeffress-greta-thunberg-rainbow-flood-climate-1461326

List of nicknames used by Donald Trump:
https://en.wikipedia.org/wiki/List_of_nicknames_used_by_Donald_Trump

Donald Trump's false equivalence of hate based neo-Nazis and those protesting against hate. Calling them all "Very fine people."
https://www.politifact.com/truth-o-meter/article/2019/apr/26/context-trumps-very-fine-people-both-sides-remarks/

Hush money, Porn Star, Stormy Daniels:
https://www.cnbc.com/2019/07/17/feds-end-probe-of-hush-money-that-trump-ex-lawyer-michael-cohen-directed.html   See also: https://www.npr.org/2019/07/18/743112028/trump-spoke-with-cohen-as-they-aides-sealed-hush-money-deals-in-2016

On family separation at the southern border of the United States:
https://www.cnn.com/2019/11/06/politics/family-separation-court-filing/index.html
And from Time Magazine. https://time.com/5710953/trump-administration-confirms-more-migrant-family-separation/

El Paso shooting and gunman's manifesto:
https://www.usatoday.com/story/news/nation/2019/08/05/dayton-ohio-el-paso-shootings-weekend-mass-killings-2019/1919633001/

Donald Trump's use of the term "invasion."
https://www.nbcnews.com/think/opinion/trump-s-anti-immigrant-invasion-rhetoric-was-echoed-el-paso-ncna1039286

Suspect: https://www.cnn.com/2019/08/05/us/el-paso-suspect-patrick-crusius/index.html

Quote "I think God calls all of us to fill different roles at different times..." made by Sarah Sanders:
https://www.huffpost.com/entry/sarah-sanders-donald-trump-is-president-because-god-wanted-him-there_n_5c52203ee4b093663f5af20a

"We have guns because it's our God-given right enshrined in the Constitution" made by Sarah Sanders:
https://www.nbcnews.com/think/opinion/trump-republicans-don-t-hate-gun-control-because-nra-they-ncna1057841

Historical timeline of the development of guns:
https://www.pbs.org/opb/historydetectives/technique/gun-

timeline/

When was the Bible written?
https://www.bbc.co.uk/religion/religions/christianity/texts/bible.shtml

When was the United States constitution written?
https://constitutioncenter.org/learn/educational-resources/constitution-faqs

"If the Democrats are successful in removing the president from office..." statement made by Robert Jeffress:
https://www1.cbn.com/cbnnews/2019/september/robert-jeffress-to-news-if-the-president-is-removed-from-office-its-going-to-cause-lasting-wounds-in-our-country

President Donald Trump Tweets Robert Jeffress's "civil war" statement:
https://twitter.com/realdonaldtrump/status/1178477539653771264?lang=en

Process for the Impeachment of United States President of the United States and removal from office:
https://www.reuters.com/article/us-usa-trump-impeachment-explainer/how-does-impeachment-of-a-u-s-president-work-idUSKBN1XV2FP

Current political profile of the United States Senate in 2019 - 2020. (116 US Congress):
https://en.wikipedia.org/wiki/116th_United_States_Congress

"Shithole Countries" Statement from Donald Trump:
https://www.washingtonpost.com/politics/trump-attacks-protections-for-immigrants-from-shithole-countries-in-oval-office-meeting/2018/01/11/bfc0725c-f711-11e7-91af-31ac729add94_story.html

https://www.nytimes.com/2018/01/11/us/politics/trump-shithole-countries.html

On family separation at the southern border of the United Stateshttps://www.washingtonpost.com/immigration/aclu-says-1500-more-migrant-children-were-taken-from-parents-by-trump-administration/2019/10/24/d014f818-f6aa-11e9-a285-882a8e386a96_story.html

https://www.nytimes.com/2019/03/09/us/migrant-family-separations-border.html

"I think God calls all of us to fill different roles at different times..." Sarah Sanders: https://www.washingtonpost.com/religion/2019/01/30/sarah-sanders-tells-christian-broadcasting-network-god-wanted-trump-be-president/

Chapter 5
Overview of Freedom of Speech in the United States: https://en.wikipedia.org/wiki/Freedom_of_speech_in_the_United_States

MIT study on Fake News in social media: https://www.theatlantic.com/technology/archive/2018/03/largest-study-ever-fake-news-mit-twitter/555104/

Fake news - what it is and how does it influences us: https://www.telegraph.co.uk/technology/0/fake-news-exactly-has-really-had-influence/

Dog whistle statement made by Robert Jeffress, *"I am not saying that President Obama is the Antichrist..."* https://www.huffpost.com/entry/obama-antichrist_n_4561761 https://www.ncronline.org/news/spirituality/pastor-obama-paving-way-antichrist

"Yesterday we had the strongest dollar in the history of our

country" - Donald Trump statement:
https://www.politifact.com/truth-o-
meter/statements/2019/aug/22/donald-trump/donald-trump-
incorrect-us-dollar-strongest-its-eve/

U.S. farmers are receiving $16 billion "out of the tariffs that we've
gotten from China." Trump claim:
https://www.politifact.com/wisconsin/statements/2019/aug/02/
donald-trump/no-china-not-paying-us-farmers-16b-through-
tariffs/

"Mexico, they took 30% of our automobile business." Trump
Claim:
https://www.politifact.com/wisconsin/statements/2019/jul/23/d
onald-trump/no-mexico-didnt-take-30-us-auto-business-trump-
cla/

"Our Economy is the best it has ever been. Best Employment &
Stock Market Numbers EVER." Trump claim:
https://www.forbes.com/sites/yuwahedrickwong/2019/07/19/ch
eap-credit-and-lack-of-competition-gums-up-the-u-s-
economy/#5b77acf050c7

Trump said that "he stopped it" when his supporters began
chanting "send her back" about Ilhan Omar:
https://www.politifact.com/truth-o-
meter/statements/2019/jul/19/donald-trump/trump-said-when-
crowd-chanted-send-her-back-about-/

Trump stated (per Twitter), *I know that we've been blocked.
People come up to me and they say, 'Sir, I can't get you - I can't
follow you. They make it impossible."*
https://www.politifact.com/truth-o-
meter/statements/2019/jul/17/donald-trump/trump-claimed-
twitter-has-made-it-harder-people-fo/

Trump claimed that The United Kingdom is "our largest (trading) partner." https://www.politifact.com/truth-o-meter/statements/2019/jun/05/donald-trump/donald-trump-said-uk-americas-largest-trading-part/

Truth/Falsehood rating per Hannity:
https://www.politifact.com/personalities/sean-hannity/

Truth/Falsehood rating per Fox News Channel:
https://www.politifact.com/punditfact/tv/fox/

"When Trump used the word "sh*thole" to describe African and other nations earlier this year? No big deal" said Robert Jeffress: https://www.au.org/church-state/julyaugust-2018-church-state-magazine/featured/the-apostle-of-trump-the-rev-robert

and: https://www.au.org/church-state/june-2019-church-state-magazine/cover-story/the-not-so-magnificent-seven-whenever

Corey Lewandowski stated, *"I have no obligation to be honest with the media."*
https://www.cnn.com/2019/09/17/politics/corey-lewandowski-the-media/index.html

Chapter 6
Kids in cages and other inhuman treatment at the southern border of the United States:
https://www.hrw.org/news/2019/07/11/written-testimony-kids-cages-inhumane-treatment-border
Additionally:
https://www.buzzfeednews.com/article/claudiakoerner/children-border-detention-conditions-immigrants-hungry

Profiting off of kids in cages:
https://www.nytimes.com/2018/06/21/us/migrant-shelters-border-crossing.html

Chapter 7
Donald Trump as some kind of spiritual savior. *"Only God could deliver such a savior to our nation"* - campaign manager Brad Parscale Stated:
https://www.politico.com/story/2019/04/30/donald-trump-evangelicals-god-1294578

What is a cult?
https://www.theguardian.com/commentisfree/belief/2009/may/27/cults-definition-religion Definitions of a cult:
https://www.christianitytoday.com/iyf/advice/faithqa/what-is-cult.html
And: https://www.merriam-webster.com/dictionary/cult

Characteristics of a Theocracy:
https://www.thoughtco.com/definition-of-theocracy-721626

Chapter 8
Secretary of the State, Mike Pompeo, stated, *"Could it be that President Trump right now has been sort of raised for such a time as this, just like Queen Esther, to help save the Jewish people from the Iranian menace?"*
https://www.politico.com/story/2019/03/22/pompeo-trump-israel-iran-1232587

Statement by Jerry Falwell Jr. : *"If you give God credit for a good president, then you've got to blame God when you have a bad one."* https://www.politico.com/story/2019/04/30/donald-trump-evangelicals-god-1294578 Falwell continued, *"God called King David a man after God's own heart even though he was an adulterer and a murderer." "You have to choose the leader that would make the best king or president and not necessarily someone who would be a good pastor."*

Statement by Sarah Huckabee Sanders: *"I think God calls all of us to fill different roles at different times, and I think that he wanted Donald Trump to become president."*
https://www.cnn.com/2019/01/30/politics/sarah-sanders-god-trump/index.html

Robert Jeffress statements: *"to resist government is to resist God himself."* https://www.mediamatters.org/fox-friends/fox-panel-attacks-church-denomination-sheltering-immigrants

"In the case of North Korea, God has given Trump authority to take out Kim Jong-Un."
https://www.independent.co.uk/news/world/americas/donald-trump-north-korea-latest-nuclear-war-kim-jong-un-god-given-authority-robert-jeffress-white-a7883746.html

Evangelical Christian Pastor, Jim Bakker stated, *"leaders of the gospel and the political conservative leaders are going to be murdered."* https://www.politicalflare.com/2019/08/jim-bakker-warns-his-followers-that-christian-leaders-and-republicans-will-die-if-trump-loses-in-2020/

Mike Pompeo, stated, *"Could it be that President Trump right now has been sort of raised for such a time as this, just like Queen Esther"*
https://www.washingtonpost.com/world/2019/11/01/trump-administrations-obsession-with-an-ancient-persian-emperor/

Sanders: *"I think God calls all of us to fill different roles at different times, and I think that he wanted Donald Trump to become president."*
https://www.washingtonpost.com/religion/2019/01/30/sarah-sanders-tells-christian-broadcasting-network-god-wanted-trump-be-president/

Chapter 9
Conservative Evangelical leader, Tony Perkins, the president of the

conservative Family Research Council states that Donald Trump gets a "mulligan."
https://www.cnn.com/2018/01/23/politics/tony-perkins-trump-affairs-mulligan/index.html

"mulligan." Tony Perkins:
https://www.washingtonpost.com/news/the-fix/wp/2018/01/23/you-get-a-do-over-here-evangelical-leaders-apparent-double-standard-on-the-alleged-trump-daniels-affair/

https://www.nytimes.com/2018/01/26/opinion/trump-christian-right-values.html

Chapter 10
The modern day hypocrisy and hijacking of "Thoughts and prayers" https://www.cnn.com/2018/02/20/us/thoughts-and-prayers-florida-school-shooting-trnd/index.html

More reading per "Grace"
https://www.christianity.com/theology/what-is-grace.html

Additional Notes

The Deepening crisis of Evangelical Christianity:
https://www.theatlantic.com/ideas/archive/2019/07/evangelical-christians-face-deepening-crisis/593353/

Evangelical leaders on the wrong side of history - on the wrong side of Jesus:
https://www.patheos.com/blogs/faithonthefringe/2018/08/the-irony-of-evangelical-idolatry-in-the-white-house/?utm_source=facebook&utm_medium=social&utm_camp aign=FBCP-CTOBM&fbclid=IwAR3Y2_juHTv7W6bHZdXV_IURv76wWMijII

yUFYB300atR9Wc-fitVLmDIvo

Do conservative pastors like Trump for his hate?
http://nymag.com/intelligencer/amp/2019/08/do-conservative-evangelicals-like-trump-for-his-hatefulness.html#aoh=15669652694050&referrer=https%3A%2F%2Fwww.google.com&amp_tf=From%20%251%24s

Is God on Team Trump?
https://www.latimes.com/opinion/op-ed/la-oe-balmer-god-and-trump-20190204-story.html?_amp=true#referrer=https%3A%2F%2Fwww.google.com&amp_tf=From%20%251%24s

Millions of Americans believe God made Trump President.
https://www.politico.com/magazine/story/2018/01/27/millions-of-americans-believe-god-made-trump-president-216537

Trump's false and misleading claims.
https://www.washingtonpost.com/politics/2020/01/20/president-trump-made-16241-false-or-misleading-claims-his-first-three-years/

NPR reports Pew Study (Per Morally Upstanding)
https://www.npr.org/2020/03/12/815097747/survey-most-evangelicals-see-trump-as-honest-and-morally-upstanding

Full Pew Study (Per Morally Upstanding)
https://www.pewforum.org/2020/03/12/white-evangelicals-see-trump-as-fighting-for-their-beliefs-though-many-have-mixed-feelings-about-his-personal-conduct/?utm_source=adaptivemailer&utm_medium=email&utm_campaign=20-03-12%20religion%20and%202020%20election&org=982&lvl=100&ite=5702&lea=1272618&ctr=0&par=1&trk=

61 percent find Trump morally upstanding (Pew Research Study)

https://www.pewforum.org/2020/03/12/white-evangelicals-see-trump-as-fighting-for-their-beliefs-though-many-have-mixed-feelings-about-his-personal-conduct/pf_03-12-20_religion-politics-00-9/

Acknowledgments

There are so very many countless, "angels" and messengers who have walked in and through my life inspiring me through word and experience. You are the relationships through which God waters this garden. I smile every time I recall our encounters and am grateful for each and every one of you. A thousand blessings. Much heartfelt thanks and appreciation also to my wife, Karin, and my children for their never-ending love, support and through whom God often speaks. I love you guys more than words could possibly express. To my many Pastors, Mentors and Spiritual guides of all walks: you all have taught me so much over the years. I am deeply in your debt. And to my brothers and sisters all around the world, both in Christ and those who view our Creator through a different lens, I love you. Keep walking in the Light. You are always in my prayers.

Thank you Kelsey Krippaehne for your eagle eye and advice in editing this book and Tessa Krippaehne for helping me publish it.

Lastly, I want to thank the unseen Power that has created all that is. Thanks to God, to my Savior, Jesus Christ for loving, teaching and guiding me always. Life is beautiful. May I spend the rest of my days contributing to your great hope and purpose that all people may one day love one another and live in the joy and peace of Your nature.

About the Author

Dean Krippaehne is a worship leader, author, musician, and music producer. His music has been heard on hundreds of TV shows, Films and in new media around the world including: The Oprah Winfrey Show, Dancing with the Stars, Duck Dynasty, The Vampire Diaries, Lucky Dog, One Life To Live, Keeping up with the Kardashians, The Dr. Oz Show and The Henry Ford Innovation nation to name a few. He has also earned gold and platinum records as a songwriter and continues to speak and teach at workshops around the country. In addition to being a worship leader in his home church in South Seattle, Dean and his wife Karin have raised three daughters and now live as proud surrogate parents to both a dog and a cat.

Also by Dean Krippaehne

Demystifying the Cue

Demystifying the Genre

Write, Submit, Forget, Repeat

Made in the USA
Las Vegas, NV
04 January 2023

64865915R00111